NUMEROLOGY

Inspiring | Educating | Creating | Entertaining

Brimming with creative inspiration, how-to
projects, and useful information to enrich your
everyday life, quarto.com is a favorite destination
for those pursuing their interests and passions.

First published in 2020 by Wellfleet Press,
an imprint of The Quarto Group
142 West 36th Street, 4th Floor
New York, NY 10018 USA
T (212) 779-4972 F (212) 779-6058
www.Quarto.com

Wellfleet Press titles are also available at discount for retail, wholesale, promotional, and bulk purchase. For details, contact the Special
Sales Manager by email at specialsales@quarto.com or by mail at The Quarto Group, Attn: Special Sales Manager, 100 Cummings
Center Suite 265D, Beverly, MA 01915, USA.

10 9 8 7 6 5 4

ISBN: 978-1-57715-199-9

Library of Congress Cataloging-in-Publication Data

Names: Fenton, Sasha, author.
Title: Numerology : your personal guide / Sasha Fenton.
Description: New York : Wellfleet Press, 2020. | Series: In focus |
   Includes index. | Summary: "All numbers have an intrinsic energy, from
   the date of your birth to the number of your home. With In Focus
   Numerology, author Sasha Fenton gives the information you need to
   understand the significance of numbers in your life, including how to
   use them to forecast outcomes and take advantage of opportunities.
   Beautiful illustrations and a framable poster combined with expert
   information make this your go-to numerology guide"— Provided by
   publisher.
Identifiers: LCCN 2019053146 (print) | LCCN 2019053147 (ebook) | ISBN
   9781577151999 (hardcover) | ISBN 9780760367384 (ebook)
Subjects: LCSH: Numerology.
Classification: LCC BF1623.P9 F46 2020 (print) | LCC BF1623.P9 (ebook) |
   DDC 133.3/35--dc23
LC record available at https://lccn.loc.gov/2019053146
LC ebook record available at https://lccn.loc.gov/2019053147

Group Publisher: Rage Kindelsperger
Creative Director: Laura Drew
Managing Editor: Cara Donaldson
Senior Editor: John Foster
Art Director: Cindy Samargia Laun
Cover and Interior Design: Ashley Prine, Tandem Books

Printed in China

IN FOCUS

NUMEROLOGY

Your Personal Guide

SASHA FENTON

WELLFLEET PRESS

CONTENTS

INTRODUCTION

Numerology is an ancient technique that uses numbers to assess the character and destiny of a person, but it can also be used to check out the nature of a new pet, business, or anything else that you can think of, as long as it has a name or a starting date that you can work with. For instance, if you opened a shop called Carnival on July 23, 2024, you would have a date and a name that you could check out.

The system is easy to understand and use, because all you need is a pen and a piece of paper, but you can also use a calculator if you find it tedious to add up lists of figures. Numerology can be used alone or combined with a simple form of astrology for the purposes of prediction. So now, let us start by taking a very brief look at the historical background of this enjoyable and easy-to-use system.

A Brief History of Numerology

Numbers are everywhere and they always have been. Even animals have an idea of numbers, especially when on the lookout for predators, because they need to judge how many there are and how far away they might be. Similarly, a predator needs to judge the number and condition of its prey and how far away it is.

The ancient Hebrews, Greeks, and Romans used number systems based on the letters of their alphabet, but the numerals that we use today came from the Arabs. Mathematics can be traced back to the need to count the bags of grain that a farmer brought to a grain store, also to the birth of town planning, building, and architecture. The ancient Greek mathematician Pythagoras (569–470 BCE) is credited as the originator of numerology, but it was already in evidence long before his time, but it was the Pythagorean Brotherhood that worked out the basics of the system that we use today. The Pythagorean Brotherhood was established in Crotone in southern Italy in the sixth century BCE.

Pythagoras

The Hebrew *Sefer Yetzirah* (the Book of Creation) is an explanation of the spheres of the Tree of Life, which relates to the way God created the universe and everything in it. The *Sefer Yetzirah* is highly complex and extremely mysterious. Here are two of the more comprehensible examples of its many verses:

Verse two: there are thirty-two ways, ten double and twelve single, which are the twenty-two letters of the Torah.

Verse three: the ten double letters are ten and not nine, ten and not eleven. The twelve simple letters are twelve and not eleven, twelve and not thirteen.

Christianity had a new interest in numerology, and it was in the *Hermetica*, which is attributed to Hermes Trismegistus. The *Hermetica* are texts from ancient Greece and Egypt that were written in the first or second century CE. The texts are designed to teach, and they discuss philosophy and belief in the way the mind works, the natural world, the divine world, the cosmos, astronomy, astrology, and alchemy. These texts used number symbols, such as the trinity of God, the Cosmos, and Man. The crusades began at the beginning of the twelfth century, and they drifted on until the Reformation finally brought them to an end in the sixteenth century. They inadvertently connected the East to the West, bringing in many ideas from Greece, Turkey, and the East, including various forms of numerology.

In the seventeenth century, Dr. John Dee, the Astrologer Royal to Queen Elizabeth I, became obsessed by the "Enoch" system of numbers, which was supposed to lead to some kind of godly power. He went off to Prague to study this subject, because he found someone there who could show him how it worked. He was also keen to escape the religious fanaticism in England at that time, which considered the "occult" to be heretical.

During the eighteenth century, the rise of the Age of Reason meant that people turned their backs on anything that smacked of superstition, religion, mysticism, or witchcraft, so numerology went underground for a while in Europe. However, it flourished in other parts of the world, especially in India, and it was the connection between India and Britain during the nineteenth century and the rise of European empires that brought it back to the West.

Toward the end of the nineteenth century, the continued interest in all things Indian, and the discoveries of ancient Egypt encouraged people to set up societies to look into these ideas. This is when the Theosophists and *the* Hermetic Order of the Golden Dawn were founded in the UK.

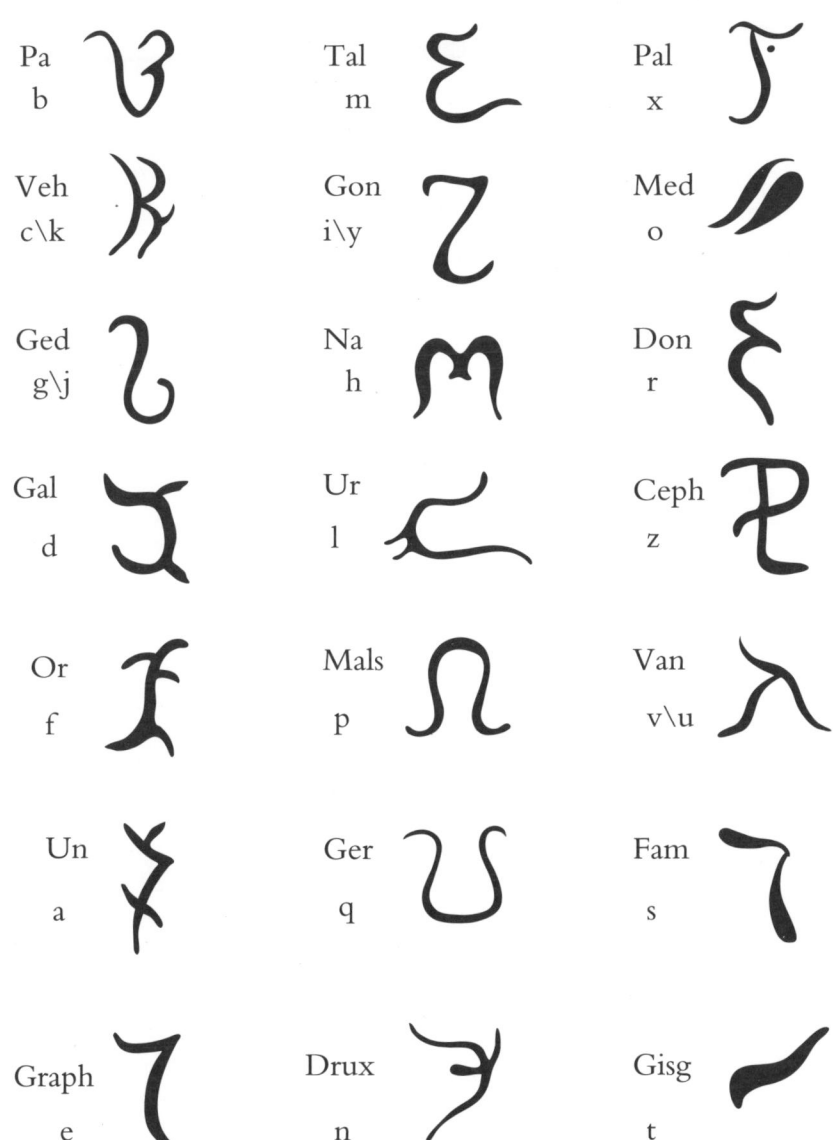

Pa b	Tal m	Pal x
Veh c\k	Gon i\y	Med o
Ged g\j	Na h	Don r
Gal d	Ur l	Ceph z
Or f	Mals p	Van v\u
Un a	Ger q	Fam s
Graph e	Drux n	Gisg t

The "Enoch" System of Numbers

In France, Napoléon Bonaparte became fascinated by ancient Egypt and by Egyptian geomancy, which is a numerical fortune-telling system. However, in France, toward the end of the nineteenth century, the palmist Cheiro and others studied everything that was weird and wonderful.

The hippie era of the 1970s brought a massive upsurge of interest in Indian philosophies to the USA and Europe, and many of these ideas have now become an accepted part of the spiritual landscape. Nowadays, those who write books or magazine articles are spreading these ideas even further—and that brings us up to date. However, today numerology is more popular in India than in the West.

Numerology Basics

Numerology is the easiest of the divinations to use because, unlike astrology, which requires the date, time, and place of birth, numerology requires only a name and a date of birth, or a name and a starting date for something. Also helpful is the fact that you don't need to memorize the rules of numerology, because you can refer to this book as you go along. However, the more you use the system, the more you will absorb, and you will soon find the character and energies that live within each number sticking in your mind.

The first part of the book shows you how to find the meanings behind the *letters* that make up a name, while the second part shows how the *date of birth* can affect a person's life. You might like to consider the day you moved into your current home or bought your car, or the day you started a new job— especially one that didn't work out well. You will be amazed at the way the nature of each place, thing, or enterprise is shown by its "birth" number and by its name.

The last few chapters show you how to forecast events by numerology, even down to the hour in which something happens. This means that you can "elect" a specific time and date in which to do something important, but life being what it is, things don't always work out so easily. For instance, a friend of mine chose the perfect date and time for her forthcoming marriage, but circumstances made that date impossible. Fortunately for her, the day that the marriage took place was also good, numerologically speaking, and the marriage is a success.

Number Basics

You are an individual who is unlike everyone else on earth, and this is reflected in the various parts of your nature. Numerology tracks this individuality by describing the different parts of your character that make up the whole. Read on and you will see how this works, and you will also see which influence is the strongest in your case.

All numbers have an intrinsic energy, and this can apply to the number on the door of your home or place of work, the number of your license plate, or any other number. Even the number on the bus or train that you routinely take to school or work can be significant. The date of birth for a person, a business, an enterprise, an event, the day you acquired a much-loved pet, or anything else that has a start date can be used with this system.

The numbers that we use are 1, 2, 3, 4, 5, 6, 7, 8, and 9. (Zero isn't used in numerology, probably because it didn't exist in ancient Greece when the system was invented.) But we also sometimes use the so-called power numbers of 11, 22, and 33, as you will see in chapter 1. A longer number will need to be reduced by adding the figures together to make a single number, which we will see below.

Important Numbers

Before we get into the subject in detail, let us take a very brief look at two of the most commonly used aspects of numerology: the Destiny Number and the Life Path Number.

The Meanings of Numbers

The meanings that are attributed to numbers 1 through 9 are the same for every type of number numerology. For example, the meaning and the energy of number 1 is the same regardless if it's the Life Path Number, the Destiny Number, or the Heart Number, and so on.

THE DESTINY NUMBER

Everything that has a name also has a Destiny Number, which we will learn more about in chapter 1. The commonly accepted description of the Destiny Number is that it shows your life's purpose and the pattern by which you will achieve it, but it can only really reflect the purpose or future pattern that your parents chose for you when you were born. That may be just fine—or it  may not. When considering your Destiny Number, calculate the names on your birth certificate and the ones you have chosen to be known by and see how both have played out in your life.

To find the destiny number of a person's name, a business, or anything else with a proper name, you take the letters in the name and translate them into numbers by means of the Alphabet Code, which we will talk about in a moment.

Which Name Should You Use?

When calculating your Destiny Number, most numerologists insist that you use your whole name as shown on your birth certificate, but there are cases where this might not be very useful. For instance, some people give their baby an official name, but then go on to call the baby something else as soon as it's born.

Where possible, use the name that is on your birth certificate, but if it isn't appropriate, use the name you started to use early in life, whether it is on your birth certificate or not. Either way, it should be the whole name, including any middle names. The birth-start name shows your destiny, but if you change your name due to marriage, for business purposes, or for any other reason, you can also check on the way this has changed your destiny.

GAMBLING

◆

If you are into horse or dog racing, you could check the animal's racing name to see whether it adds up to a winning number. Its stable name may have a completely different vibe, but that isn't the name it races under. Casinos love to suggest that 7 is a lucky number, and Chinese culture loves the number 8, but Western numerology doesn't think much of number 8, as it links with the dour and limiting planet, Saturn. Some people have a lucky number that follows them around with no particularly numerological or astrological logic behind it, whereas others have an unlucky number that they do their best to avoid.

Names, the Alphabet Code, and Important Numbers

The Alphabet Code allows you to translate the letters of your name into numbers. The aim is to end up with a whole number that is between 1 and 9. (Again, there are exceptions for 11, 22, and 33, which are called *power numbers*, but we will look at them later in this book.)

The Alphabet Code

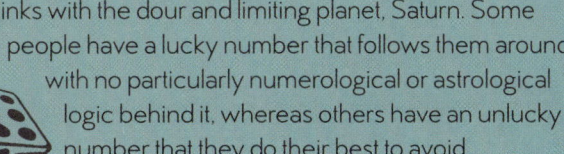

1	2	3	4	5	6	7	8	9
A	B	C	D	E	F	G	H	I
J	K	L	M	N	O	P	Q	R
S	T	U	V	W	X	Y	Z	

Let's use the example John Smith.

Total numbers for John Smith: $1 + 6 + 8 + 5 + 1 + 4 + 9 + 2 + 8 = 44$

Now we reduce the 44 to a single number: $4 + 4 = 8$

John Smith's Destiny Number is 8.

Here is a longer name I made up to show you how to deal with a more complex situation:

Total numbers for Gervaise Horatio Brown:

$7 + 5 + 9 + 4 + 1 + 9 + 1 + 5 + 8 + 6 + 9 + 1 + 2 + 9 + 6 + 2 + 9 + 6 + 5 + 5 = 109$

Reduction: $1 + 0 + 9 = 10$

Reduction: $1 + 0 = 1$

Gervaise's Destiny Number is 1.

MANY NUMBERS IN A NAME

The Destiny Number is the starting point, but there are other important numbers that you can find by adding up the vowels of a name, the consonants of a name, or the first letters of a name, or you can look at the number that appears the most often in a name. You will discover how to work these out and to understand their meanings later in this book.

The Life Path Number and Significant Dates

The Life Path Number is an important number for a person, and it can be used to make forecasts about their future. To find the Life Path Number, you add up the dates in a person's birthday. (See chapter 7 for an in-depth look at Life Path Numbers.) For example, let's say there's a person named John Smith whose date of birth is November 23, 1994. November is the eleventh month, so we start with 11 by adding $1 + 1$, followed by the rest of the date, so the complete task works like this:

$1 + 1 + 2 + 3 + 1 + 9 + 9 + 4 = 30$

Then we reduce this to a single number: $3 + 0 = 3$

So John Smith's Life Path Number is 3.

You can use the same method to find a number to represent a significant date. For example, let us assume that a wedding took place on April 18, 2017. April is the fourth month, so the figures work like this:

$4 + 1 + 8 + 2 + 0 + 1 + 7 = 23.$

Then we reduce this to a single number: $2 + 3 = 5$

So the significant number for the wedding day is 5.

Tip

It doesn't matter whether you express your birth date the way we do in the UK, the way it works in the USA, or by various other methods, because the numbers will always come to the same total. For example, someone born on the July 4, 1985, adds up as follows:

UK style: 4/7/1985—adds up to 34
USA style: 7/4/1985—adds up to 34
Other style, type one: 1985/4/7—adds up to 34
Other style, type two: 1985/7/4—adds up to 34

The 3 and 4 will need to be added together to find the Life Path Number, which in this instance is 7.

FORECASTING BY NUMBERS

To make a forecast, you need to find the Life Path Number, and add up the numbers of your date of birth, and then reduce them to a single number.

❋ ❋ ❋

Enclosed Numerology Wall Chart

Included in this book is a wall chart that serves as a quick and handy reference guide containing a summary of the essentials of numerology from the following pages.

PART I

NUMBERS FROM NAMES

1

THE DESTINY NUMBER

The Destiny Number, also sometimes called the Expression Number, comes from the number in your whole name. This shows your life's purpose and they way you go about achieving it. Here, again, is the Alphabet Code, and an example of how to arrive at someone's Destiny Number.

The Alphabet Code

1	2	3	4	5	6	7	8	9
A	B	C	D	E	F	G	H	I
J	K	L	M	N	O	P	Q	R
S	T	U	V	W	X	Y	Z	

Example—Elvis Aron Presley

Elvis: $5 + 3 + 4 + 9 + 1 = 22$

Aron: $1 + 9 + 6 + 5 = 21$

Presley: $7 + 9 + 5 + 1 + 3 + 5 + 7 = 37$

Let's put the numbers together: $22 + 21 + 37 = 80$

Reduce the numbers: $8 + 0 = 8$

Therefore, Elvis Presley's Destiny Number is 8.

Number 8 is associated with ambition and a great deal of hard work, leading to success and often to wealth. This number also belongs to those who are good to their parents, and all this was certainly true for Elvis.

Tip

The characteristics listed for each number are links between the number and other systems of divination and spiritual belief as well as the way ancient numerologists felt about the numbers.

Destiny Number 1

Characteristic: Extrovert
Astrological connection: The Sun, Leo
Symbol: The lion
Element: Fire
Similar to: Base chakra
Kabala: Unity, wholeness, totality
Best days of the month: 1, 10, 19, 28
Key concepts: Ego and personal identity

Positive Traits

- Takes action
- Initiative
- Assertiveness
- Inventiveness
- Leadership qualities
- Independence

- Willpower and determination
- Courage
- Individuality and originality
- Executive abilities

- Strong drive to achieve
- Purposeful
- Tenacious

Negative Traits

- Overassertiveness
- Selfishness
- Aggressiveness

- Willfulness
- Boastfulness

- Egotism
- Impulsiveness

The number 1 is the number of achievement, activity, power, and leadership. It is one of the strongest numbers in the list, but it can lead to a lack of compassion or patience with those who aren't as quick, clever, successful, or capable. At worst, it can make you a successful businessperson but a poor parent.

A number 1 person is bold and powerful, with strongly masculine qualities. This number is pioneering, the first in line, dominant, original, and independent. The downside is that this can lead to domineering and selfish behavior that can easily turn to aggression. It is wonderful when you use your powers of invention to get things done, to help others or to protect those you love, but it isn't good when you use your strength to bully others.

This number shows that you may have been dominated and bullied as a child. One or both parents may have thought they were always right, possibly due to religious beliefs, and they may have put pressure on you to perform or conform to their ideal. The upside of this is that you turn into a hardworking and ambitious person who is especially suited to self-employment or to reaching the top in a profession. The downside is that you may seek to dominate others in your turn. Alternatively, you may become anxious and fearful of the future. If you can find someone who will love you and give you the emotional support you need, you can overcome this and become successful in life. Others value you for your honesty, generosity, humor, and sense of adventure.

You love your children and will go the extra mile for them, but you also want them to be well-behaved and to succeed in life. When relaxed and away from work, you can be great fun and very good company.

Destiny Number 2

Characteristic: Introvert
Astrological connection: The New Moon, Cancer
Symbol: The crab
Element: Water
Similar to: Sacral chakra
Kabala: Division, relatedness
Best days of the month: 2, 11, 20, 29
Key concepts: Feeling and caring

Positive Traits

- Ability to work with others
- Fond of partnerships
- Sensitive
- Team worker

- Balanced
- Cheerful
- Cooperation
- Kindness
- Tact and diplomacy

- Peacemaker
- Mediator
- Modesty
- Sincerity

Negative Traits

- Timidity
- Anxiety
- Lack of confidence

- Depression
- Leans on others

- A worrier
- A miser

The number 2 implies duality. It represents the quality of nurturing a seed that has been planted. It represents a drive for harmony and balance, a need for a feminine yin to balance the masculinity of yang. It is passive, intuitive, receptive, and emotional. This number is about partnerships and relationships, so the chances are that these traits will be important to you.

There may have been considerable tensions in the childhood home, and this might lead you to develop a hard shell, and childhood events may result in the kind of insecurity that leads you to become penny-pinching and miserly. You may seek to acquire goods in order to make yourself feel safe. Even if you don't go to this extreme, you will probably always be careful with money and possessions.

On a positive note, you are keen on family life and will be fiercely loyal to loved ones, and you will even carry the habit of loyalty through to those you work for. You are not a natural leader because you prefer to help others and to be appreciated for what you do. You may choose to work in one of the caring professions such as in the health field, or you may be interested in complementary health and energy healing.

Destiny Number 3

Characteristic: Extrovert
Astrological connection: Mars, Aries, or Scorpio
Symbol: The ram
Element: Fire
Similar to: Throat chakra
Kabala: Fertility, completion
Best days of the month: 3, 12, 21, 30
Key concepts: Creative and adaptable

Positive Traits

- Optimistic
- Joyful
- Sociable
- Friendly
- Inspiring teacher
- Idealistic
- Good at explaining things
- Kind
- Outgoing
- Creative and possibly artistic
- Intuitive with good insight
- Intelligent
- Versatile
- Charming
- Enjoys life

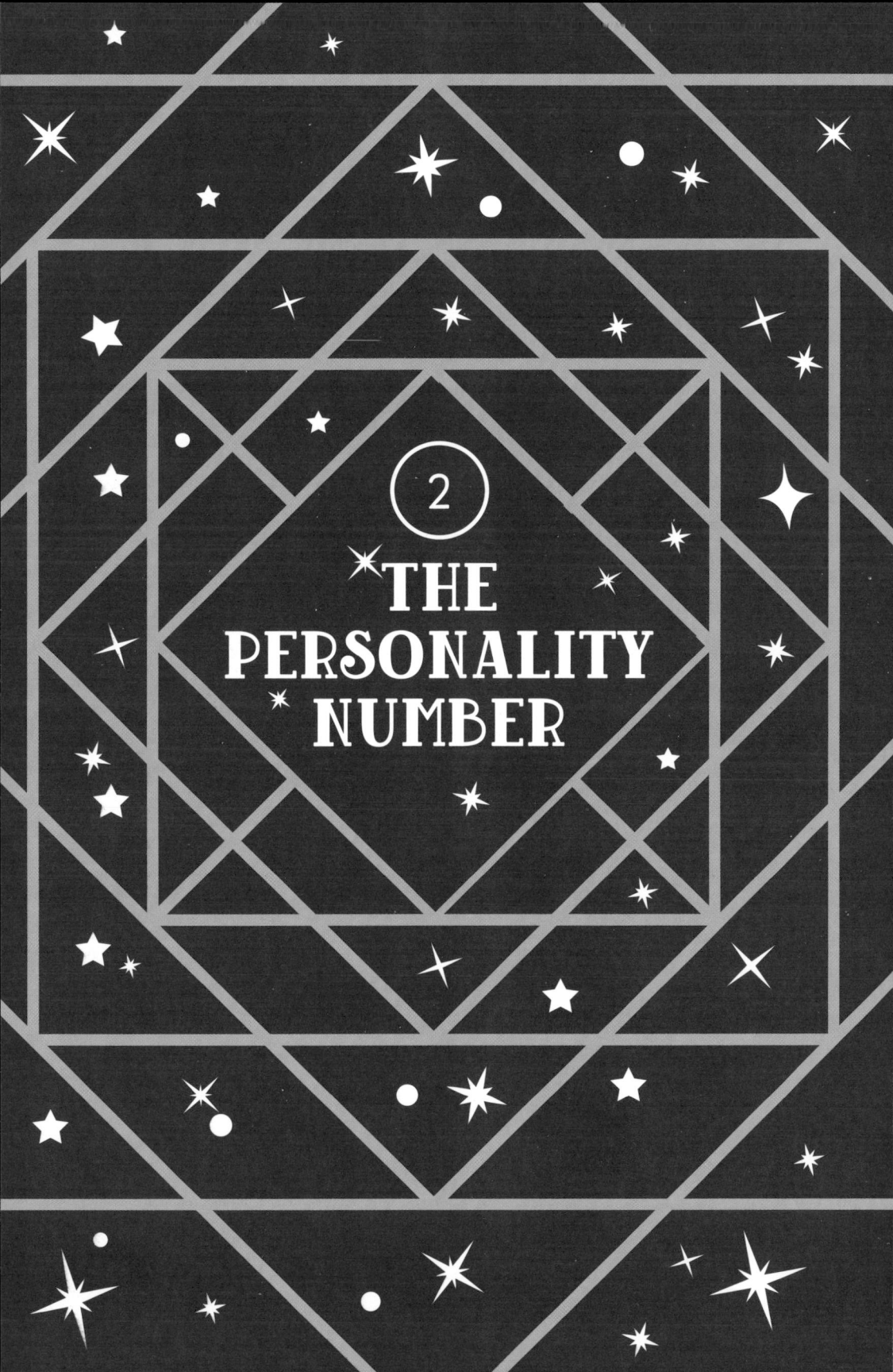

2

THE PERSONALITY NUMBER

The Personality Number, which some call the First Impression Number, represents the outer personality, which may have developed out of the programming you received at home, at school, and in your society when you were young. You find the Personality Number by adding the consonants in your name and ignoring the vowels. It is best to use the name you usually call yourself when calculating this number.

The Alphabet Code

1	2	3	4	5	6	7	8	9
A	B	C	D	E	F	G	H	I
J	K	L	M	N	O	P	Q	R
S	T	U	V	W	X	Y	Z	

Here is an example for someone called Olivia James. Ignoring the vowels, the consonants in Olivia's name are L, V, J, M, S.

This works as follows:

L	3
V	4
J	1
M	4
S	1

The total for Olivia is: $3 + 4 + 1 + 4 + 1 = 13$
Reduction: $1 + 3 = 4$
So Olivia's Personality Number is 4.

Let's take a look at what the different Personality Numbers mean.

Negative Traits

- Self-centered
- Moody
- Impulsive

- Arrogant
- Boastful
- Tends to exaggerate

- Good starter but poor finisher
- Scattered energies

The number 3 represents creative enterprise and growth. This number suggests that material benefits will come to this person. You may have a desire to act or you may love music, but your circumstances wouldn't have encouraged you to do these things when you were young.

You probably found it difficult to stand up to your parents, and you may have a problem with authority figures throughout life. The result is that you may fluctuate between being charming and accommodating, or stubborn and irritable, when dealing with others. Despite a difficult start and the wrong kind of education or career, you do well in your chosen profession. You are an explorer and may be restless and fairly easily bored, so you are best suited to a job where you can get around and meet a variety of people. You love travel, and your holidays are the highlight of your year, as this is when you can leave your mundane life of home and work, socialize with other people, and see other places. It is also where you can stretch your imagination.

Some of you do well in business, either by working for a boss who appreciates you and allows you to do things your way, or by owning your own business. You are an excellent salesperson with the persistence needed to follow up a lead. You are also obliging to others, which is always a good thing in a job or in business. Another positive aspect is that you love to read and learn, and you can be a good teacher or guide to others.

You may be extremely lucky in your choice of friends and colleagues, and other people will be happy to help you whenever they can. You are sociable and flirtatious, and you enjoy having a good time and seeing others enjoy themselves. You are kindhearted and have good intentions, but your innate selfishness and moodiness can ultimately spoil your relationships.

Destiny Number 4

Characteristic: Introvert
Astrological connection: The Earth, opposite
   the Sun on a horoscope chart
Symbol: Downward pointing triangle
Element: Earth
Similar to: Base and sacral chakras
Kabala: Solidity, reliability, the law
Best days of the month: 4, 13, 22, 31
Key concepts: Common sense and materialism

Positive Traits

- Practical
- Scientific mind
- Good organizer
- Good eye for detail
- Good memory
- Puts down roots
- Sense of order
- Struggles against problems
- Upholds the status quo
- Hardworking
- Logical
- Realistic

Negative Traits

- Shy
- Slow
- Stubborn
- Argumentative
- Fixed opinions
- Confused thinking
- Dour and serious
- Unimaginative
- Materialistic

The number 4 signifies the earth and the physical and material world, and it represents a foundation that a person can build upon, because 4 is the number of form and shape. Like the four legs on a table that keep it stable, the number 4 represents balance, stability, and security, but it also symbolizes restrictions and limitations.

You have common sense and will listen to reason, but you seek to control the environment in which you find yourself. Logical thinking and systematic work methods belong to this number. Your childhood should have been a happy one with plenty of love and support from family and teachers, but later in life you may get into the habit of leaning on others and treating them as replacements for your parents or teachers. You will always be a hard and reliable worker with a sensible attitude to whatever you take on, and while you are a loyal employee, you can also succeed in a business of your own. You may be somewhat unimaginative, but you make an excellent financial advisor or

craftsperson, and over time, you build up a great fund of knowledge, while your capacity for hard work can make you rich.

You are a loyal and loving family person, and you are sensitive to those you care about. You may not be glamorous or exciting, and you may be shy and hesitant in coming forward when it comes to asking someone to go out with you. You are happiest when in a settled relationship, and you are a loyal and dependable family member. Your downside is that you may be somewhat dull, stuck in your own routine and a trifle unbending, controlling and a bit too serious for your own good or your lover's.

Destiny Number 5

Characteristic: Mostly extrovert
Astrological connection: Mercury, Gemini,
    or Virgo
Symbol: The twins
Element: Air
Similar to: Throat chakra
Kabala: Life, creativity, growth
Best days of the month: 5, 14, 23
Key concepts: The mind and education

Positive Traits

- Versatile
- Humorous
- Tolerant
- Lively
- Creative and artistic
- Quick thinking
- Eager to learn
- Loves to travel and explore
- Visionary
- Good communicator
- Can be drawn to writing or teaching
- Likes to be constructively busy
- Sociable

Negative Traits

- Bad-tempered
- Dissatisfied
- Easily bored
- Restless
- Makes decisions without enough forethought
- Obstinate and unwilling to listen
- Moody and temperamental
- Unable to finish what has been started

The number 5 shows the need to break out of the enclosed structure that is signified in the number four. This number breeds activity because it hates routine and restriction, and it becomes nervous and restless when held down. It hates to see its freedom threatened because it needs a wide area in which to move around and to express its drive and energy.

You seek constant change and variety, and the scope to put the fruits of physical and mental experiences into action. This may be physical changes of scene, but it can also be mental stimulation that comes from the world of ideas or interests. This number is associated with social contacts, education, ideas, and communications of all kinds.

Your parents were reasonable and your childhood fairly happy, but there were events that made you feel very insecure. Your parents may have been sick, or they may have been refugees from another country, or they may just have moved around a lot, which meant that you could have gone through several changes of home or school. You may tend to walk away from problems rather than face them. Your desire for the admiration of others may lead you to become a success in sports or the media. You are clever and versatile, so you need a number of different challenges in your job, you accept the ideas of others as long as they are sensible, and you are a good leader because you allow others to do their jobs without undue interference. You couldn't live with a boring partner for long.

Destiny Number 6

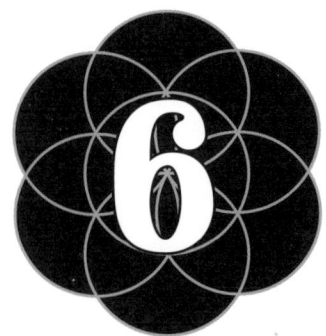

Characteristic: Introvert
Astrological connection: Venus, Taurus,
   or Libra
Symbol: The bull
Element: Earth
Similar to: Heart chakra
Kabala: Fruitfulness, harmony, domestic life
Best days of the month: 6, 15, 24
Key concepts: Harmony and peace

Positive Traits

- Humanitarian
- Responsible
- Kindhearted and
  compassionate
- Charitable
- Balanced
- Creative
- Good imagination
- Sympathetic
- Unselfish
- Good to family
- Good domestic skills
- Nurturer

Negative Traits

- Obstinate
- Easily flattered
- Pompous
- Self-righteous
- Outspoken
- Meddling
- Dominates family
  members

The number 6 is associated with feelings and emotions. It also relates to the home, family life, and the person's upbringing. It rules the ability to love others and to care for a family. This number represents responsibility for others and providing them with food, warmth, love, and security. It relates to all that is beautiful and harmonious, especially in the areas of giving, caring, and looking after the health of others.

You felt extremely insecure when young and may have had parents who either did not communicate or gave you strangely mixed messages. Your mother may have had some sensible things to say on some occasions, but also odd fixed ideas that may not have been normal or logical. Your family venerated hard work, and you may have sought to impress them and to win their approval by working hard, even as a child. The outcome is that you become a tireless worker in adult life, possibly wearing yourself out for the sake of others. Your family and employers might appreciate and value you for the effort that you

make, but they may take the credit for your work and the profits that should be yours to keep. You can normally be relied on to achieve all that you set out to do, but your chief fault is perfectionism. You have an excellent mind and also a powerful desire to make the world a better place.

Destiny Number 7

Characteristic: Introvert
Astrological connection: Neptune, Pisces,
    and to some extent the Full Moon
Symbol: The two fishes
Element: Water
Similar to: Brow chakra
Kabala: Mysticism, magic, spirituality
Best days of the month: 7, 16, 25
Key concepts: Intuitiveness and spirituality

Positive Traits

- Intelligent
- Sensitive
- Intuitive
- Studious
- Perfectionist
- Good at details
- Good at science
- Good researcher
- Can be religious or spiritual
- Likes to be alone and to meditate

Negative Traits

- Likes own opinion
- Cold and sarcastic
- Very reserved
- Self-righteous
- Takes offense at small things and when none is intended
- Hides his or her motives

The number 7 represents two ideas that are linked, and the first is the need for rest, relaxation, and time off to think things through and time to allow thoughts to drift aimlessly. After a while, the thoughts take shape and something useful will emerge. The second idea is that of spiritual significance, as this encompasses the kind of reflection, analysis, and inward journey that leads to enlightenment of both a practical and spiritual nature. In essence, this is a meditative number. It can be the sign of an inventor, because your mind is attuned to science, ideas,

mathematics, and knowledge, in addition to spirituality.

You probably had a fairly easygoing relationship with your parents and other adults when you were a child, partly because you are reasonable, sociable, and pleasant. You turn your amiable nature to good advantage in both your career and your personal relationships, but you need to guard against a tendency to let opportunities pass you by. You must avoid sitting back and allowing others to make progress at your expense or to take what should rightfully be yours. You prefer thinking to acting, and you tend to sit back and observe the world and what's going on around you. You may become a philosopher, a mystic, a researcher, or an artist. You are wise but you may not cash in on your talents and wisdom or achieve much in practical terms. You need to develop your artistic or spiritual talents and also find practical life partners and business partners.

Destiny Number 8

Characteristic: Extrovert
Astrological connection: Saturn, Capricorn, and to some extent Aquarius
Symbol: The goat
Element: Earth
Similar to: Solar plexus chakra
Kabala: Material concerns, leadership, justice, ambition
Best days of the month: 8, 17, 26
Key concepts: Ambitious and self-sufficient, powerful karma

Positive Traits

- Executive ability
- Leadership skills
- Good judgment
- Decisive
- Persistent
- Hardworking
- Successful and possibly wealthy
- Could succeed in politics
- Can support a cause

Negative Traits

- Overambitious
- Works too much
- Impatient
- Irritable
- Can be a bully
- May not care much about others
- Becomes overtired and stressed
- Materialistic

The number 8 suggests material success but also spiritual attainment. There has to be progress in both areas, and a balance needs to be maintained between them. This karmic number shows that we reap what we sow, and it indicates a mastery over the physical world and an acceptance of responsibility.

Childhood may have been uneasy due to a disinclination to conform, and you may have had a parent who was obstinate, dictatorial, rigid, or absent. If your home life was all right, you may have been overdisciplined at school, so you may have become crafty and cunning to survive. Later in life, you may become domineering, dictatorial, or rigid, although you also learn to use charm to get what you want.

You are extremely intuitive and can sum up people and situations in a flash. Add this to shrewdness, intellect, organizational ability, and a capacity for hard work, and it is easy to see that you can make a tremendous success of your chosen career. You may become wealthy and much admired by others. You will have high status and a good opinion of yourself. You are an excellent salesperson who has the persistence to promote both goods and services and to follow up any potential business lead.

You may become domineering in later life, and you may even come to view your personal relationships as a kind of power struggle, or you may end up being dominated by someone else. If you can learn to be tolerant of those who are not lucky enough to be born with your strength and courage, you will make your loved ones happy and in turn become happy yourself. You need to ease up a little and learn to relax and enjoy life.

Destiny Number 9

Characteristic: Mostly extrovert
Astrological connection: Jupiter, Sagittarius,
    and to some extent Pisces
Symbol: The archer
Element: Fire
Similar to: Crown chakra
Kabala: Humanitarian, inspirational leadership
Best days of the month: 9, 18, 27
Key concepts: Compassion, knowledge, and karma

Positive Traits

- Sociable
- Outgoing
- Kind and friendly
- Artistic with literary talent
- Creative
- Humanitarian
- Compassionate
- Knowledgeable
- Capable
- Talented
- Unselfish
- Good-natured
- Spiritual

Negative Traits

- Vain and boastful
- Seeks flattery
- Wants attention
- Possessive
- Bad-tempered and moody
- Loses money and goods
- Unsettled and unable to finish things

At best the number 9 incorporates all the previous numbers, so it represents completion and true love of the highest order. This shows that a certain point has been reached, although there are always higher levels to aspire to. The soul is old, but there is always something more to learn.

Your parents encouraged you early in life, and this could lead to success in your own field. You need to explore the world of ideas, which could link to the realms of education or hobbies and interests that give you an opportunity to look at things from a variety of angles. In many cases, the visionary aspect of your nature can lead to an involvement in religion, philosophy, or the spiritual life, and you could go on to inspire others.

You love to travel, so you could end up seeing a fair bit of the world, while using your talent for getting along with all types of people. This can bring success in an artistic or a sporting endeavor or in business, but you may simply drift along without achieving very much.

Power Numbers

When assessing the personality by the Destiny Number, there are three other numbers that numerologists consider, and some call these "power numbers," because they may have a stronger influence on a person than the single numbers do. The power numbers are 11, 22, and 33.

If a name or a date adds up to one of these numbers or reduces down to one of them, you can choose to look up their meanings and leave it at that, but you can also then reduce the power numbers until you end up with a single digit, which will give you something extra to check out.

An interesting case is the number 4, which concerns a person's land, property, and maybe a small business that could be run from the home, while the number 22 is connected with architecture, civil engineering, construction, and so on, which is similar but on a much larger scale.

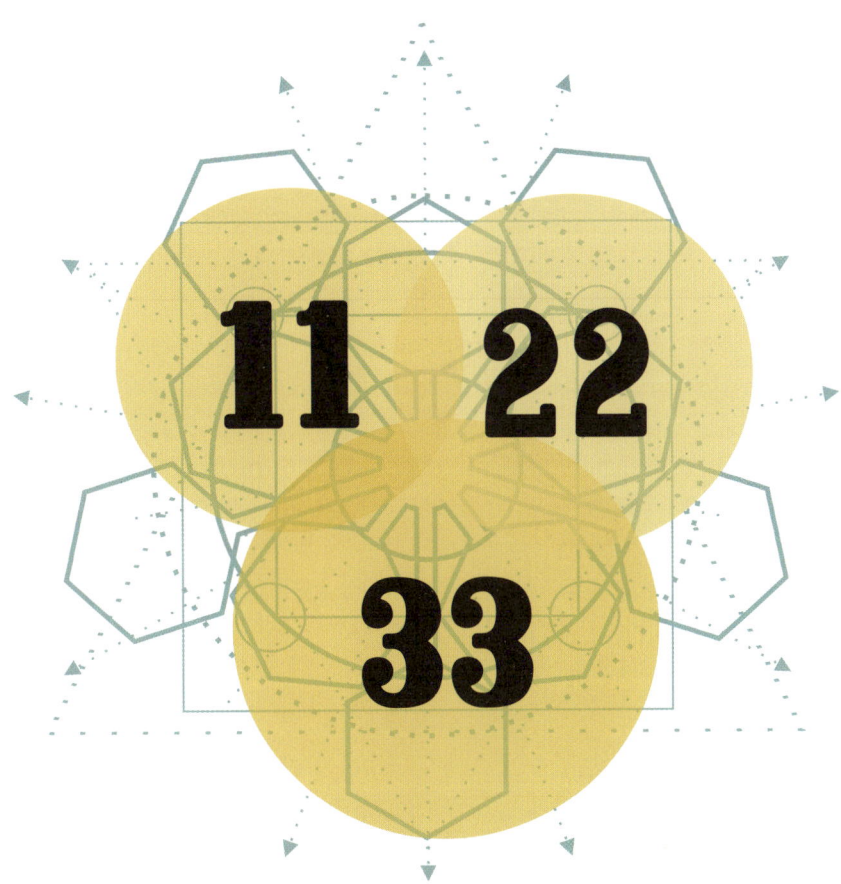

Destiny Number 11

Positive and Negative Traits

- Desire for justice
- Self-absorbed
- Unconventional
- Rigid

The energy behind the number 11 is of justice, of fair play and of strength that is used wisely. There are times when it is right to administer justice, but others when it is right to sit back and wait things out. The trick is to know which is which.

Your childhood was reasonable, but something made you keen to distance yourself from others. You may have distrusted adults or other children or been disinclined to listen to anything others had to say. You started out by being quiet and serious, but later you may have become opinionated, inflexible, and difficult, and it is possible that you are hiding an inferiority complex under an arrogant, uncaring, or defiant attitude. If you find the right career outlet for your talents, and develop sensitivity toward others, you will become less self-absorbed. You have a good mind and some original ideas, but you are attracted to unconventional ideas and an unconventional lifestyle, so marriage, children, and a routine family life may never hold any appeal.

Destiny Number 22

Positive and Negative Traits

- Exceptional ability to create or build things
- Good with young people
- Sharp tongue
- May be a bully

There is an element of justice that must be applied here, because you may receive unjust treatment during the course of your life, but you must strive to be fair in your dealings with others. There is a feeling of completion here, with just rewards for all that has been done before—perhaps in a previous life. You could have loved and admired your parents, or you could equally have feared their strength and domination, but either way, you develop an independent attitude with an unusual outlook or nonconformist view of life.

You could become an excellent counselor and guide to younger people, but you are even more in tune with the structure of materials, which could lead to a career in building, architecture, civil engineering, or even in sculpture or art. If you can control your tendency toward angry or wounding outbursts or a tendency to dominate others and not allow them to have their own way from time to time, you can succeed in a relationship. You could be very helpful to a lover who needs to be guided and cared for.

Destiny Number 33

Positive and Negative Traits

- Very spiritual
- Sympathetic
- Lonely
- Similar to a hermit

This is a difficult number in which loneliness and hardship will occur, but these experiences bring enlightenment and an ability to sympathize with the plight of others. Charitable work, doing things for others, and self-sacrifice have a part to play here, but there is also the development of a strong inner world of spirituality and artistry. You can be practical and very successful, but you will always rush to help others. If you develop your artistic talents and work quietly on your own projects, you can achieve considerable success.

You may have been isolated during childhood, possibly due to sickness and stays in the hospital, and this leads you to tap into the world of imagination, and when storms threaten later in life, you will still be able to escape into a dream world of your own making. Your parents were not particularly hard on you, but life and circumstances made you a little fearful.

You are likely to work in one of the caring professions or take up religious or spiritual work where you help others. The danger here is that you become overwhelmed by the needs of others and end up drained and exhausted.

Personality Number 1

You appear confident, outgoing, and friendly, but you hide any feelings of insecurity. You may be arrogant or overbearing and demanding, and you won't allow others to criticize you. You are also hard-working, capable, generous, and successful, and you will ensure that your family has a good home to live in.

Personality Number 2

You appear to seek harmony and peace, and avoid confrontation, yet despite this, others still think they can have a go at you when they feel like hurting someone. You can be too much of a perfectionist, which makes you hard for others to cope with. Learn to relax and let fools think what they like.

Personality Number 3

You have a cheerful and outgoing outer persona that appears confident and popular, but you might not be nearly as secure as you pretend to be. You can be extravagant and over-the-top in some of your behavior, but your energy and sense of fun win others over. Take care not to be boastful or conceited in an attempt to hide a somewhat low self-esteem.

Personality Number 4

You like to appear steady, reliable and loyal, hardworking, and decent. You make a trustworthy and dependable lover. You are a bit too conservative and unwilling to explore the world or take on a challenge or do something new. Expect others to have their own ideas and let them be whatever they want to be.

Personality Number 5

You are intelligent and inquisitive, well read, and a fund of knowledge and information—and you are happy for people to see you that way. You are great fun to be with and are a good friend. You may travel for work or fun, and you may move from country to country during your life. You love novelty and can be restless. Don't pass on gossip.

Personality Number 6

You strive for harmony and hate arguments, and trouble can upset you badly. You like to look good and you adore beautiful things, so you can overspend on luxury items. You appear gentle, charming, and good company, but your desire to have nothing but the best can make you selfish.

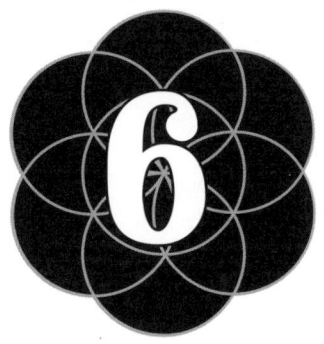

Personality Number 7

You don't have a great outer manner as you can be cool at best—and snobbish, hard to get to know, and inclined to sneer at others at worst—but beneath this unpleasant outer manner is a decent person waiting to get out, and you can actually be an interesting and loyal friend. You tend to be into mystical or offbeat matters, and you can be very intuitive. You may get along better with children than with adults.

Personality Number 8

You are determined to be seen as a success with a wealthy lifestyle, so you probably overwork and overdo things in order to create this image. You are likely to be a success in your work and a good employer, with organizational, sales, and financial skills. You want the best of everything for yourself and family. You can be bossy and hurtful toward others.

Personality Number 9

You love to be seen as a free spirit who is great fun, with a magnetic and sexy persona. You have many lovers, which is fine as you would be a failure in a standard relationship. You need your freedom and can't be restricted by work or love. You never turn up anywhere on time. You are spiritual, somewhat mystical, and possibly also religious.

Personality Number 11

You like to be seen as a steady and reliable person who has a secure personal life, good relationships and loyal friends. At work or in the outside world, you can behave unpleasantly to others. When you realize you are being unfair and start helping colleagues and validating their work, your own career starts to prosper.

Personality Number 22

You want to be seen as a capable builder or gardener, and there is no doubt that you are good with material things, so you might be great at do-it-yourself projects. You are helpful and like others to consider you as someone who has good judgment and counseling skills. You are a cheerful person and good fun as a friend.

Personality Number 33

You appear to others as charitable and compassionate, but you do have a strong desire to help those who are weaker than you are. You may love animals or strive to improve the lot of the poor. You are extremely spiritual and a really good person, but you must guard against being worn out by people who are looking for someone to take care of them.

※ ※ ※

3

THE HEART
NUMBER

The Heart Number, or Soul Urge Number, talks about the inner personality, the individual's true motives and hidden talents. For this we look at the vowels in a name. In this example we will use Alexander Collins.

The Alphabet Code

1	2	3	4	5	6	7	8	9
A	B	C	D	E	F	G	H	I
J	K	L	M	N	O	P	Q	R
S	T	U	V	W	X	Y	Z	

Ignoring the consonants, the vowels in Alexander's name are A, E, A, E, O, I.

A	1
E	5
A	1
E	5
O	6
I	9

So the total for Alexander's vowels comes to 27.

Reduction: 2 + 7 = 9

So Alexander's Heart Number is 9.

Here is what the different Heart Numbers mean:

Heart Number 1

Your inner nature is ambitious and purposeful, so you want to make a success of business or politics, or both. You are confident and inspire confidence in others, but you may spend so much time trying to be successful in your business or career that you neglect your family and your love life.

Heart Number 2

Your real nature is generous, with a kind heart and a desire to care for others. You may work as a healer, therapist, palmist, or something of the kind. Inwardly you are very vulnerable and need comfort and security from a partner or lover.

Heart Number 3

You have some hidden fear of failure or of looking weak and being rejected, but you should put this aside because you do have real talent, and you make a reliable partner and a good friend. You have a great sense of humor.

Heart Number 4

You are a born homemaker and a real family person who is happiest in the home. You need comfortable surroundings and do much to improve the appearance of your own home. You don't like being in the spotlight and can be crippled by shyness. You are sensitive and easily hurt.

Heart Number 5

Your inward nature is studious, you may be a good linguist, and you love to read and learn. You need freedom and can be restless. You dislike authority figures, but you enjoy friendship and are good to your friends. Love relationships are rarely easy for you, though, as they may be too restrictive.

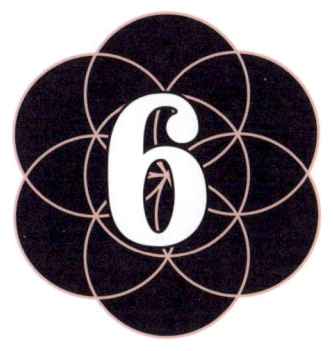

Heart Number 6

You are your own worst enemy as you criticize yourself and lack confidence. However, you are often the mainstay of your family and friends, and you always put the needs of others first. You need lots of praise and support and a partner who doesn't suddenly turn on you and hurt you. It may take a long time for you to find the right partner.

Heart Number 7

You like to be seen as mystical with special knowledge that isn't available to ordinary people, so you may be into religion, mysticism, and philosophy, and you may prefer the world of ideas to the world of people. You may walk away from those who seek to tie you down.

Heart Number 8

You would make a wonderful salesperson and could become a real tycoon, because you are a good organizer and like to be in control of events. You find it hard to relax and can lose your temper when things go against you. You prefer to be at work than resting, but you do need to take time off.

Heart Number 9

You are a great mechanic and can solve problems that others can't even see. You need variety, a change of scene, and something to challenge you. You may not be so successful in personal relationships, though, and your partner will need to understand this about you.

Heart Number 11

You like to rely on yourself and you don't trust the judgment of others, so you make your own decisions and stick to them. You have a strong sense of justice and can be idealistic. You can make yourself useful to others, and you love feeling needed.

Heart Number 22

You have an inner need to create beautiful things and those that work on a practical level, so you may be drawn to work in architecture, building, farming, or civil engineering. You can make a success of a career and be a great friend. Relationships work well as long as you have peace in the home.

Heart Number 33

Loving kindness is your middle name, and you want to help others. Your values are spiritual rather than materialistic and you are very generous. You should avoid people who would drain you and give nothing back.

✳ ✳ ✳

4

YOUR HIDDEN PASSION NUMBER

Some people are so laid-back that they don't feel passionate about anything, but many of us have a hidden passion or some psychological need that we keep under wraps. You can find yours and those of your loved ones by making a note of the number that comes up most often in your name. To some extent, this is not the fairest aspect of numerology, because numbers are derived from letters. Anyone who relaxes in the evening by playing Scrabble will tell you that the most common letters in the English language are *vowels*, with E being the most common. However, where names are concerned, that isn't always the case, as you will see in the example that I have used for this chapter. So now, let us use the Alphabet Code once again to look into the hidden recesses of the personality of an imaginary person called Thomas Hatherleigh.

The Alphabet Code

1	2	3	4	5	6	7	8	9
A J S	B K T	C L U	D M V	E N W	F O X	G P Y	H Q Z	I R

Thomas Hatherleigh

T	2	H	8	1	Three occurrences
H	8	A	1	2	Two occurrences
O	6	T	2	3	One occurrence
M	4	H	8	4	One occurrence
A	1	E	5	5	Two occurrences
S	1	R	9	6	One occurrence
		L	3	7	One occurrence
		E	5	8	Four occurrences
		I	9	9	Two occurrences
		G	7		
		H	8		

Interestingly, Thomas has all the numbers contained in his name, with 8 being the most common, so number 8 is Thomas's Hidden Passion Number. If two numbers are equally common, it shows a personality with two distinct sides, and you need to check out both. Now that you know how to find Hidden Passion Numbers, let's see what they mean.

Hidden Passion Number 1

You want to be a leader and you want others to see you as special. You may dream of winning at a sport, being a success in business, winning a trophy, or doing something that puts you on a pedestal. You want to do things your own way and would love to prevent others from having power or influence over you.

Hidden Passion Number 2

You would love to be in a happy marriage-type relationship in an atmosphere of harmony, and you may achieve this if you are lucky. At your job, you want to work on a scientific or creative project with others, and you love to help others, but you would love it if they were grateful for the help you give them. If you could give up your boring job and work in the world of art, music, fashion, or the media, you would be ecstatic, but are those jobs open to you?

Hidden Passion Number 3

You might have a secret desire to be an actor, which could take you into a hobby that requires you to learn lines and take center stage, such as amateur dramatics or freemasonry. You would love to be a confident, outgoing, charming, and amusing salesperson or someone who can promote goods and services. Most of all, you want others to admire you and to like you.

Hidden Passion Number 4

If you are a hard worker, it might be worth considering why you put in so many hours and make such an effort, especially if the eventual outcome is going to benefit someone other than yourself—say, the owner of the business or the board of the school or hospital or whatever. The chances are that you would love it if your boss and your colleagues told you that the workplace would fall apart without you. Being more organized and efficient than others pleases you. In your personal life, you want to be seen as the one who provides for the family's needs.

Hidden Passion Number 5

Wouldn't it be nice if you could afford to take off and travel the world? If you could at least have one interesting trip a year, you might be able to see something of the world. Some of you long to write novels or children's books, but this takes more determination and grit than you might actually have. When change and uncertainty come along, you manage better than most, because that is when your dislike of boring routine works in your favor rather than against you.

Hidden Passion Number 6

You long to help anyone or anything that is in distress and to spend at least some of your time solving the problems of others and putting the world to rights. You would love to be a counselor, teacher, or veterinarian, and you wouldn't mind putting yourself last when it

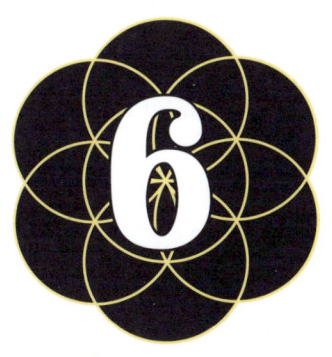

comes to fulfilling the needs of others. The deep, hidden desire at the back of all this compassion and self-sacrifice is for others to acknowledge your goodness and strength and to love you in return for all that you do for them. Take care they don't just use you and walk away laughing at you.

Hidden Passion Number 7

You would love to spend your time considering the deeper meanings of everything, and looking into areas of spirituality that fascinate you. You have a lot in common with philosophers of the past who spent years researching the numerical system of Enoch or the Kabala in the search for God and all his works. You would love others to consult you for answers, so it wouldn't be surprising to find that you are into astrology, numerology, or the like.

Hidden Passion Number 8

You want to be rich and successful and to be seen as a major player on the world's stage. You need to do great things and to use your ideas, capacity for hard work, and entrepreneurial spirit to become someone others envy and admire. Part of this is driven by a need to be wealthy and powerful enough to prevent others from putting you down. Part of it is materialism—the need to have a nice home and expensive possessions.

Hidden Passion Number 9

You would love to put the world right, which might take you into something like local government, where you can see the results of your efforts. However, some of your dreams and desires will be so high-minded and so great that you may have difficulty even getting anything off the ground. You would love to be less emotional and to be seen as "cool," but this is hard for you to achieve.

Power Numbers

The power numbers aren't used in this area of numerology, probably because this wasn't part of the original Pythagorean system, but something that was discovered later on and subsequently absorbed into numerology as a whole.

✳ ✳ ✳

5

HIGHER NUMBERS

Numerology has some ancient ideas that are interesting, despite having a limited amount of use, such as the Higher Numbers. They are included in this chapter in case you would like to experiment with the system. Add up the numbers in your name until you reach a number that is between 10 and 30, but do not reduce it down to a single digit. Afterward, look up the interpretation, but be aware that some may find these interpretations old fashioned or even harsh.

If your number is too low or too high to work within this system, just skip this chapter; there are plenty of other systems in this book that you can use instead.

The Alphabet Code

1	2	3	4	5	6	7	8	9
A	B	C	D	E	F	G	H	I
J	K	L	M	N	O	P	Q	R
S	T	U	V	W	X	Y	Z	

Delia Ann Beaufort

D	4	A	1	B	2
E	5	N	5	E	5
L	3	N	5	A	1
I	9			U	3
A	1			F	6
				O	6
				R	9
				T	2

The total for Delia is 67.

Reduction: 6 + 7 = 13

So Delia would look up the number 13 for her reading. *(In normal forms of numerology, we would reduce this to 4, but not in this particular method.)*

Higher Number 10

This is a number of power that can be used for good or evil, so you may overreact to situations one way or another. It is the number of extreme responses and overreactions, but used wisely, this could be a powerful individual.

Higher Number 11

There are two forces operating here and they may work together or they may bring happiness, but they could cause separations, divorces, and disunity and problems of an unusual kind. You must avoid treacherous people.

Higher Number 12

If someone puts you in charge of a large matter or enterprise, you should consider why you are being given the opportunity, because it may not be all that it appears to be. You should avoid being too self-sacrificial or becoming a victim.

Higher Number 13

This is a good number that leads to power, authority, and high status, but it also brings unexpected ups and downs. You are a pioneer who has many new and original ideas but could also become selfish and destructive.

Higher Number 14

You may be a lucky gambler or someone who makes a success of a job in travel or some form of journalism or writing. Business partnerships are all right as long as you use your intuition before jumping into things and don't take too much on trust.

Higher Number 15

You are a charismatic person who is charming, pleasant, and good at making others happy. Tradition says the subject with this number should keep away from such things as magic and witchcraft in order to avoid being hurt by these things.

Higher Number 16

Although successful, you need to take great care before climbing ladders or taking chances as you can be accident prone. However, vivid dreams or an inner voice can give warnings and therefore save you from danger.

Higher Number 17

This number talks about good karma and a peaceful life, with a certainty of reaching heaven at the end of it. It links to ancient wisdom, mysticism, and love. You can overcome problems at home or at work, and you will be happy.

Higher Number 18

Love conquers all in the case of this number, as it is the only thing that is able to deflect a host of problems, both within the family and in the world as a whole. Interestingly, you may gain financially due to some kind of weird political situation or things that go on in your environment.

Higher Number 19

This is a happy number that ensures all enterprises and activities will meet with success. It guarantees victory and the ability to get over loss and failure. Luck surrounds you, and there is an aura of happiness, joy, and a fulfilled life.

Higher Number 20

This number is great for personal success and happiness, but it isn't wonderful for business. You need to be ready to tackle major obstacles in life and not to back off from challenges. It represents action and activity.

Higher Number 21

Victory and achievement are represented here, so you can be sure that all efforts will meet with success. You will overcome problems and reap karmic benefits, even though it may take a while before this happens.

Higher Number 22

You must avoid seeing things through rose-colored glasses, as things may not always be as clear-cut as they seem. There may be people who are untrustworthy or even up to no good in your immediate surroundings, so avoid putting your trust in them.

Higher Number 23

There is an aura of success here, as you can expect success and happiness in your career and love life. You will overcome problems and be able to call on the help of people in high positions to protect you or help you on your way.

Higher Number 24

As long as you don't get too big for your boots or overspend on luxuries, you can expect success in legal matters, creative work, and relationships. You are attractive, well liked, and loved, but should not neglect spiritual life.

Higher Number 25

Although there may be a difficult start to life, you overcome it and become a success in the long run. You learn as you go along and put the lessons of life to good use, especially when common sense and judgment are required.

Higher Number 26

You are unselfish, compassionate, and helpful, but may find that others take advantage. You should be very careful about taking advice from others, as it could bring disaster.

Higher Number 27

If you use your brains, success and financial reward will follow, but you must strive to finish what is started. Good use of imagination will lead to success and a rise to a high position as long as you ignore criticism born of envy.

Higher Number 28

You can become successful as long as trust isn't placed in the wrong hands and if competitors don't cause damage. If losses are incurred, you will start from the bottom again, doing things better the second time around.

Higher Number 29

You may not have the best love life in the world, and you can make a mess of work if you put your trust in useless friends. Trouble will come but it can be overcome, and as long as you keep your spirits up and believe in yourself, you will succeed.

Higher Number 30

You are something of a hermit or a loner, but this might be a temporary condition that can change later. You depend on yourself but also on the universe and the spiritual world. You may make a success of life, but in a quiet way, and alone rather than in a crowd.

6
THE LIST OF FATES

Some attribute the List of Fates system to Pythagoras, but others maintain that its origins go back much further, as they are part of the secret knowledge Moses brought out of Egypt during the Exodus. The question of origin aside, the List of Fates is based on the letters of the alphabet, and the system doesn't require any special skills other than the ability to add up the numbers. Each letter is ascribed a numerical value from 1 to 1400. In theory, you should use the name as it appears on your birth certificate as that is said to be the fate that you were born with, but I am a great believer in using the name you use now and with which you are comfortable, so maybe try the system with your birth name and any subsequent names.

The List of Fates Alphabet Code

A = 1	G = 7	M = 30	T = 100
B = 2	H = 8	N = 40	U = 200
C = 3	I = 9	O = 50	V = 700
D = 4	J = 600	P = 60	W = 1400
E = 5	K = 10	Q = 70	X = 300
F = 6	L = 20	R = 80	Y = 400
		S = 90	Z = 500

At first glance it seems strange that the letter J is ascribed a value of 600 coming as it does between 9 and 10, and that W has a value of 1400 when it is between 700 and 300. The List of Fates was based on early Hebrew and Greek alphabets, so I guess that's why the order of the letters is weird to us.

Tip

You will notice some numbers have links to planets, but these are not linked to normal astrology as we know it, so I believe the connection goes back to ancient times.

Character and Fate

This is based on the letters in a person's name, so write down the name in full and put the number beside each letter as shown below. When you have added all the numbers, don't reduce them to a single digit as you do in normal numerology. If the final sum comes to more than 1,300, which is the highest number with an interpretation in the list, eliminate the first figure and use only the remainder. For instance, if you end up with 1,740, reduce this to 740 and go from there.

For example, take the name Maisie Anne Dixon:

M	30	A	1	D	4
A	1	N	40	I	9
I	9	N	40	X	300
S	90	E	5	O	50
I	9			N	40
E	5				

Maisie Anne Dixon's name adds up to 633 but this number doesn't appear in the List of Fates, so we break it down into those that do appear. In Maisie's case, these are 600, 30, and 3.

House Numbers and Other Numbers

If you live in a house or apartment or work in a place that has a street number, the List of Fates could provide a guideline to what your fate will be while you are there.

Planets, Planetoids, Asteroids, and Signs

There is a kind of cosmic combination that rules these numbers. Some of these stellar objects were known to the ancients, but others have become tacked on to the number system in subsequent millennia.

The List of Fates

1 Mars, the God of War, is associated with this number, so this belongs to an ambitious person who will stop at nothing to get what they want. The person is forceful, domineering, arrogant, argumentative and determined, but also very successful. This could be a captain of industry or a military leader.

2 An eclipse of the moon is linked to this number, which means that the subject will achieve great wisdom due to a difficult karma. Suffering and grief can mark this number, but the person does find the strength to cope with it.

3 Jupiter is connected to this number, so these people think deeply and look into belief systems and spirituality. They have a strong belief in ethics, justice, and religion. This number is also associated with travel and luck.

4 This number is associated with the earth, so the person's nature is sensible, practical and reliable. These folk are wise and realistic, and they work hard and get on well in life as a result. They are slow and thorough, but they get there in the end. They are devoted to their families and their homes.

5 Mercury is associated with this number, so it links to using one's hands to make a living as well as using intelligence. There is a connection to health and healing, so this person may work in a caring job but could equally work in sales, marketing, broadcasting, or journalism. This person might have a somewhat nervy or neurotic nature.

6 This number is linked to Venus and conveys an appreciation of beauty and a sense of fashion and style. The person is refined, tasteful, and decorous; has a beautiful home; and can put on a gourmet meal that looks and tastes beautiful. The subject is both creative and a perfectionist, so anything he or she makes is very attractive.

7 This person is governed by the full moon, which makes them somewhat spiritual, caring, protective of others, and somewhat psychic. There is a dislike of restriction and a love of freedom, but as long as these individuals are left to get on with life in their own way, they will be very happy.

8 These subjects are ruled by Saturn, which gives them strong opinions and a powerful nature. They like justice and fair play and want to do things properly and to be seen as decent and honest. They may work too hard at times and may expect too much of themselves. There are times when these folks may feel that they aren't up to the job, or that they are struggling along on their own, but they are very capable.

9 These individuals are ruled by a particularly aggressive Mars influence, which makes them impulsive and bad-tempered. They may be impossible to please, so personal and business relationships are bound to be difficult, and there may be business failures and financial hardship as a result.

10 A combination of Saturn and the sign of the Capricorn are in charge here, so there will be good times and bad ones, but the general tone will be a gradual "goat-like" climb to success. The subject has a good mind and is a rational thinker. He or she will be happier and more successful later in life than in early life.

11 The difficult side of Uranus rules here, so if these subjects put their mind to work and achievement instead of picking fights, they could be very successful in work and in personal relationships. They can't admit to being wrong and won't apologize or make restitution for the hurt they do to others.

12 The restless planet Neptune, along with the adventurous planet Jupiter, join forces to set the scene here, so these individuals should live in a city or in a busy environment, because that is where fortune will smile most on them. They will travel a fair bit and connect with foreigners for business and pleasure. These folks are cheerful, generous, sophisticated, and fond of a change of scene or of new ideas. They will have a happy and lucky life.

13 A particularly difficult eclipsed moon, along with the sign of the Cancer, rules this number. These people had a difficult early life and may have been badly treated in an early relationship, so they carry a chip on their shoulders. They don't care about spirituality and trust little other than money, goods, and things they can keep for themselves.

14 There is an asteroid called Lilith that can turn up both in astrology and in this ancient form of numerology, and when it does so, it makes the individual's early life very hard to cope with. I have looked into this in both astrology and numerology, and the theory works. This person is landed with a situation in which he or she needs to work off bad karma that belonged to a previous life. They may have to learn about God and the universe and also find a way of making sacrifices to clear their karmic debt before they can be happy.

15 Mars and Venus combine to focus the subject's attention on their body, so looks, appearance, and the physical body are important here, and the person may be a body builder or someone who strives after physical perfection. He or she must guard against going too far and becoming muscle-bound or anorexic. It is possible that the person is vain, but it is equally possible that they never think they look good enough.

16 The planet Venus and the sign of Libra can bring luck, love, happiness, and abundance, but it can also make the person lustful, selfish, and luxury loving. At best, this subject is a wonderful lover, but at worst a Don Juan type who doesn't care about anybody's feelings. The individual is attractive, sexual, and likely to have many sexual adventures during their life. They may inspire jealousy in others.

17 Neptune can blind people to reality and Saturn can be a hard master, and it seems that the difficult side of both of these planets is in charge here, so the individual must guard against being used by others or being swindled. This is not a good omen for business and financial matters.

18 The sign of Sagittarius and the planet Jupiter can have a difficult effect on a person's childhood and youth. The subject learns to put on a tough exterior that hides a soft center. The toughness is a form of self-preservation in response to bad behavior from those who should be caring and loving toward this person but who let them down time after time.

19 The planet Mars and the sign of Aries sometimes exert a weird kind of senselessness, and it is the case with these folks. They are clever and even academically gifted, but they lack common sense and will make silly decisions. They shouldn't gamble in business or in any other way to do with money matters. They might chase after the wrong goals or choose the wrong friends.

20 There is a lunar influence here, but it seems to be hidden behind the clouds, because like the number 2 that this number derived from, this number may lead to poverty and loss, unhappiness and hopelessness. These subjects need to find a way through this, and put the past behind them, and then find something worth living for. This will take courage and dogged determination.

21 Pluto and the sign of Scorpio rule this number, so these individuals are intelligent, deep thinkers, and very perceptive, but like to keep their thoughts and feelings to themselves. They may be so self-protective and so hard to get to know that those who try to form relationships with them soon give up.

22 The idealistic planet, Uranus, and the sign of Aquarius are in charge here, so these individuals are idealists who want to put the world to rights. One may be an eco-warrior, another may be someone who fights hard for underdogs. These folks want the world to be perfect and may find it hard to live with the fact that it isn't. They may even become some kind of martyr.

23 Mars and Saturn can be difficult planets, and it seems that they combine here to create a small-minded person who can see only their own narrow point of view and won't allow anyone else to have an opinion. They are materialistic and can't abide any spirituality or any philosophy other than their own.

24 The happy planet, Jupiter, and the sign of Sagittarius rule here. These subjects will have interesting lives, because they are happy to try anything new and fascinating. They will travel and meet a variety of people, and they may be daring explorers who go to places and do things that normal people would avoid. They learn a lot, but they aren't good at settling down and having a normal family life.

25 Neptune and the sign of Pisces can endow a person with amazing powers, so this is a highly intelligent person with a powerful imagination and an open mind. This person can see beyond what is obvious and can even visualize the future. He or she is creative and very clever.

26 The sun rules this number, as does the sign of Leo, so this person is a useful member of any team but, in reality, is a born supervisor and possibly something of a whip-cracker. He or she gets the job done and won't put up with delays or excuses. Their job is likely to be tough and unglamorous, but vital to the economy.

27 The better side of Pluto rules this number, because these subjects are idealists who look for causes to fight for; they are courageous and even heroic. They will choose a tough life, possibly in the military or a responsible job, such as police officer or firefighter. They don't choose an easy life but enjoy what they do because it is useful to the community.

28   A combination of the sun and Venus can have a strange effect on an individual, and that seems to be the case here, because these subjects love to be in love and are happiest when being taken over by passion and problems associated with love. They are in love with the idea of love, which makes them pretty much unable to live in a normal relationship or a normal domestic situation. They have a need to be overwhelmed by emotion.

29   The planet Mercury and the sign of Gemini rule communication, so here we find communicators who want the world to know what they think. They may tweet their views every day or go into a job where they can air their views professionally, such as in broadcasting, journalism, or politics.

30   The sign of Pisces and the planet Neptune can have a difficult affect, which seems to be the case here, because these people aren't likely to be successful in marriage-type relationships as they find it hard to stay true to any lover. Indeed, they may be married several times. Professionally, they are likely to become popular and even famous, either because they look for fame or because it somehow finds them.

31   The sign of Leo and the sun can make a person work hard for what they want, and this is the situation here, so fame, fortune, and the respect of others can be the fate of this person, but it will be something they work hard to achieve. These individuals drive themselves and push others as well, but they may not give themselves the credit they are due.

32   The sun and moon can join forces to make this subject kind, loving, successful in romantic relationships, and happy within a family. He or she also does well in business, probably due to their ability to work in harmony with others.

33   The planetoid Chiron is a secondary ruler to the sign of Virgo, and this combination rules this number, because the person is somewhat idealistic and unworldly, so will probably work in a job that involves taking care of vulnerable people or maybe looking after sick animals. This person may not be practical or sensible and may have worries and fears that have no real foundation.

34 Mercury can make a person neurotic and anxious, and that is the situation here. The subject is a worrier who makes molehills into mountains. He or she needs to find ways of relieving inner stress, such as meditation, spiritual healing, relaxation therapy, sound therapy, and so on.

35 Venus can make a person keen to keep their body in good shape, so these individuals head to the gym on a regular basis. They are pleasant folk who try to create an atmosphere of harmony at home and at work.

36 Pluto and Uranus combine to make a very clever person who takes up large projects and succeeds at them. He or she may be a groundbreaking scientist who thinks big.

37 The sign of Leo rules this person, so he or she is happy, normal, and pleasant and wants nothing more than a happy family, a decent job, and an ordinary life. This person should get all they want in life.

38 The malefic sides of Capricorn and Scorpio combine to make a nasty person who should try to avoid being spiteful and hurtful to others. They want to be rich and successful, and are greedy, but life rarely gives them the wealth and renown they crave.

39 This number is ruled by the original and interesting sign of Aquarius, so this is a successful person who will invent something wonderful or make some kind of breakthrough that improves life for everybody. This person is a revolutionary in the nicest sense of the world and deserves the praise and respect he or she gets from others.

40 Saturn can lead a person to reach a high position in life, only to become embroiled in a scandal that destroys all they have achieved. They will be controversial and possibly notorious, and they may get into a mess of their own or one made by those around them.

41 The downside of the sign of Virgo can have a strange effect, which can be seen in this number. So the subject can do well in life but may be the architect of their own downfall through selfishness and greed, choosing the wrong friends, or behaving badly. They may never learn from their mistakes or even understand why they upset others so much.

42 The sign of Gemini and the planet Saturn can combine to create a pessimistic misery whose life is probably not good. These subjects see everything in shades of gray and seem to draw trouble onto themselves.

43 Mercury is the planet that rules here because it makes a person curious and interested in everything they come across, so this subject is a student of everything that interests them.

44 The powerful combination of the sign of Leo and the better side of the planet Saturn can combine in some way to make a person a great success, so this person will achieve fame, glamour, and the adulation of others. He or she may become very high and mighty and a legend in their own lifetime, living in a gilded palace with all the trappings of power and wealth. Traditionally, this number was associated with royalty.

45 Mercury and Venus make this person a good orator. He or she may become a politician that the public likes and trusts. These folks get on with everybody, regardless of their background, and will do well when dealing with groups and crowds.

46 Agriculture is influenced by several planets, but the fact that the number 46 reduces down to 1 makes Mars the most important planet in this case. Farming, growing things, or even having a large family is possible, and the individual is practical and sensible while also being inventive. Over time, this person should become quite prosperous.

47 This number is linked to the sign of Taurus and also to the moon, so a pleasant life filled with contentment and joy characterizes this number. Life may not be exciting, but it will be happy and fulfilled.

48 The sign of Libra, with its image of a pair of scales, rules these individuals, so they are drawn to justice and the law and may work in the legal field. They may seem unemotional and calculating, and it will take time for them to work out whether people are worth knowing and worth accepting into their life.

49 The sun can make a person too materialistic, as can Saturn, so these planets rule here, because this person will acquire property, money, savings, and possessions. He or she may become afraid of losing what they have amassed.

50 There is a downside to the signs of Pisces and Sagittarius that seems to be in charge here, so there is no point in expecting this subject to find a job that lasts a lifetime or to commit to a relationship. This person isn't interested in solving anybody else's problems or getting involved in anything for long. They might spend some part of their childhood in the wrong school or spend some time in the hospital, which makes them determined to avoid being trapped again.

60 A combination of Venus and Pluto can bring intense love relationships, but also intense loss. This subject will suffer a painful parting at some time, and tradition says this is the number for widowhood, but it could be down to divorce or enforced parting of some kind. This person has to find a way of living with loss and sadness.

70 Mercury and Uranus combine to show how science, poetry, invention, and intellect attract these subjects, who spend their lifetime learning and acquiring knowledge. They are refined, tasteful, and intellectual. They may become inventors who design something useful.

75 The adventurous sign of Sagittarius rules this subject, so he will travel far and wide and may become something of an explorer. These folks are happy to be among people of different backgrounds from their own, even extremely primitive people of some kind. They are more concerned with the world as a whole than local problems.

80 These subjects are ruled by the energies of Chiron and the sign of Aquarius, so they are idealists who want to put the world to rights. They may be drawn to finding cures for diseases and won't be put off by the size of the job, so will spend their life achieving much in this field.

81 This can be a combination of Neptune and Pluto, because there is something strange and magical here. The person might be a gifted medium or even a stage magician. He or she may become a specialist of some kind who can find answers to obscure questions.

90 This number is ruled by the malefic side of the sign of Aries, which makes the individual self-centered and selfish. This person can't see their own faults and is unconcerned by the needs of others.

100 This mixed bag seems to be linked to a combination of Mars and the full moon, because although this person has many blessings and can be on the receiving end of many karmic benefits, not everything in his or her life is easy to live with or to live up to.

120 Mars and the moon are in charge here, so the subject could be a military person, a politician, or both. He or she is patriotic and may have a romantic feeling about their country.

200 The signs of Libra and Pisces are both inclined to make their subjects ditherers who can't make up their minds. This person could get ahead in life if only he or she could choose a path forward and stick to it.

215 Pluto is clearly ruling this sign because some kind of major crisis will happen during this person's life, and it could be due to a war, famine,

earthquake, hurricane, or some other uncontrollable event.
He or she should just about be in the right place to escape calamity,
perhaps with a crowd of people who manage to get away in time.

300 Jupiter can bring bolts of light, which seems to be the case here
because these subjects are religious or have some political belief that
rules their life, possibly due to some kind of epiphany. Once their
beliefs become formed, they won't be tempted away from them.

318 The sign of Gemini is clearly in charge here, as this person is a
communicator who has an important message to spread to the wider
world. Nothing will stop him or her from trying to get their message
across to others, so this person may become the prime minister or
president of their country.

350 Taurus can make a person fight for the things he or she considers to
be right. Other people or circumstances may make it hard for these
individuals to keep on fighting for their chosen cause, but they will
take it up again and keep going with it as soon as they can.

360 The happy side of the sign of Cancer seems to rule these folks, as they
are fond of family life and are also patriotic. They don't spend time
pursuing causes, though, preferring a pleasant, quiet life listening to
music and pottering around in the home or garden.

365 The planet Chiron is associated with teaching and learning, so it has
a major influence here. This is an academic who might be into science,
history, astronomy, astrology, or anything else of a mental nature.
This person can deal with normal daily life but prefers to study and
become an expert in his or her field.

400 The signs of Capricorn and Scorpio can link with karmic debt,
which seems to be the case here. This person's early life may
be tricky, but he or she manages to get over it and become a
traveler who goes on some kind of spiritual journey at some
point in life.

490 This number is ruled by the enquiring sign of Sagittarius, so this individual is a seeker who wants to know the meaning of life and will explore many faiths and different civilizations in the quest for answers. This person may travel in search of the truth and might find some interesting answers along the way.

500 The planet Jupiter and the sign of Sagittarius ensure that this is someone who grows up in a faith, only to jettison it later when they find something that makes more sense to them. This individual will spend their lifetime on the path to enlightenment and may become a senior leader in some kind of religion before long.

600 The sun and Mercury rule these subjects because they want the best of everything. They search for the best job, the best home, the best education for their children, and the best possessions. They are perfectionists who may be interested only in the finest antiques, the finest goods, and the finest lifestyle.

666 According to legend, this is the "number of the beast." The planet might be a malefic Mercury, because the number relates to a dishonest person who has a cunning and calculating mind. This person may plot against others and doesn't do much good for anybody.

700 The sun and Chiron suggest a courageous person who fights for what is right and what is good, so this person fights on even when the odds are unfavorable, and usually wins in the end. This person is strong-minded, opinionated, and determined to be the best and the most successful in whatever battle he or she takes on.

800 The planet that is associated with this person is the sun, because he or she won't allow anything to stand in their way. He or she could become a top politician, a true empire builder, a top businessperson, a celebrity, a film star, or anything else that makes them rich, famous, and successful.

900 Like all the numbers that reduce down to 9, the miserable side of Saturn has a powerful influence here. A childhood of poverty and deprivation leads these individuals to do all they can to overcome hard times and become successful. They may live through a war situation or some other kind of difficulty but will overcome it all. Unfortunately, they are aggressive, touchy, quarrelsome, uncivil, and unpleasant, so their personal relationships will fail unless they learn to rein in their difficult nature.

1000 The good side of Mars is evident here, because this high-minded individual is moral and merciful. He or she may be religious or spiritual but even if not, they still strive to be a good person.

1095 Some distant planet such as Sedna rules here because this is the sign of the hermit. This person is reclusive and may be a specialist who works from home or a small office, working on inventions or interesting projects. These folks don't socialize much and avoid personal relationships, as they prefer to think and to ponder on life, the universe, and everything.

1260 These subjects are ruled by the signs of Cancer and Scorpio,  because they can't leave their past behind so they dwell on past hurts or past problems. They may carry a burden of guilt around with them or may hate those who have hurt them. They find it hard to move on.

1300 The truly karmic planets are Saturn and Pluto, so these are in charge here, because the subjects will be on the receiving end of hatred due to their religion, beliefs, race, color, ethnicity, or something else that attracts discrimination. Attacks on their beliefs or origins will only make their pride in their background and their faith and beliefs that much stronger.

✳ ✳ ✳

PART II
NUMBERS FROM BIRTH DATES

7

THE
LIFE PATH
NUMBER

The Life Path Number is so well known that everyone who is into numerology learns how to use it. It has older roots than the Life Number, which you will see in the next chapter, but both are relevant, so you might want to add the information in this chapter to what you learn in the next chapter to make a fuller reading for each number.

You can find your Life Path Number by adding up the numbers in your date of birth. To understand what these numbers mean, you will find a brief explanation below, but for a deeper one, please turn back to chapter 1.

For example, if you were born on June 7, 1987, you would calculate your birthday as follows:
6 + 7 + 1 + 9 + 8 + 7 = 38
Reduce this: 3 + 8 = 11
Reduce this: 1 + 1 = 2

This would make you a number 2 but also a number 11, which is a power number in numerology, so both numbers would apply. If you get an 11, a 22, or a 33 as part of your calculations, use that number as well as the number it reduces down to.

Life Path Number 1

Characteristics: leadership, strength, and authority

You are strong, creative, and practical, and you excel in a position of leadership where you get others to put their shoulders to the wheel. You would excel in an important job, either working for or running a large enterprise.

Life Path Number 2

Characteristics: partnerships and harmony

You are happiest when in harmonious partnerships or with like-minded people. You are sensible, cheerful, and keen to serve the needs of others, perhaps in a political arena.

Life Path Number 3

Characteristics: restless but an effective worker

Travel for work or pleasure matters, while boring routine jobs will be given to others to do. You need to be able to come and go without being questioned. Being sensible, and fairly psychic, you can achieve success.

Life Path Number 4

Characteristics: practical and sensible

You work hard in a steady and methodical manner and may place high value on traditional methods, but you also may buck tradition and start a revolution. While being reliable, you can also be nit-picking and too materialistic.

Life Path Number 5

Characteristics: communications, travel, and foreign connections

You communicate for a living, so you may be a salesperson, a travel agent, a teacher, or a writer. You love seeing new places, but you also need the security of a home and family to come back to.

Life Path Number 6

Characteristics: self-sacrificial, helpful, gentle, and dreamy

You want a peaceful life, but you may sacrifice too much and hand over too much power to business partners, bosses, and lovers. You can succeed in the arts or writing or the entertainment industry, or some form of mental or physical healing.

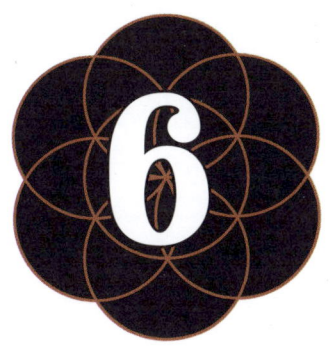

Life Path Number 7

Characteristics: good imagination and into spirituality

You have powerful intuition, sensitivity, and a mediumistic nature, which lead you into religion or spiritual matters. You are probably artistic and creative, but you aren't interested in hard work unless it is for a creative or spiritual purpose.

Life Path Number 8

Characteristics: leadership, salesmanship, attraction to business

You can succeed at anything you put your mind to, but your failures can be pretty spectacular. You work hard and aim to be fair and honest, but ambition may bring hardness and insensitivity. You may become a powerful tycoon, a success story, but you can attract envy.

Life Path Number 9

Characteristics: into religion, spirituality, and the arts

You are compassionate, loving, and spiritual but can become too involved in cults, religions, or other forms of rigidity. You are probably into antiques, beautiful furniture, music, art, the theater, and creative pursuits.

Life Path Number 11

Characteristics: likes partnerships but also personal success

You are an unusual person who can achieve great things, and you are intuitive enough to take chances on business matters. You mean well, but can be selfish, and while you can make a great success of something, you can spoil it by becoming lazy and self-indulgent.

Life Path Number 22

Characteristics: works on big projects

You may be a talented builder, architect, or engineer, but while leadership skills are apparent, a bullying manner could ensure that you aren't liked. You take family responsibilities seriously and can enjoy the company of children.

Life Path Number 33

Characteristics: an unusual and very saintly person

You may choose to become a priest, a nun, or just a very spiritual person, and you want to give everyone who needs your help unconditional love. Despite all your goodness, you could be lonely, probably because your many companions try to take advantage of your kindness and ask too much of you.

✳ ✳ ✳

8

THE LIFE
NUMBER

The Life Number is much the same as the Life Path Number because it is derived from the birth date. However, it is a less familiar concept that became tacked onto basic numerology at some time in the past. It is surprisingly useful because it gives a quick reference to the birth date numbers—this is handy for those occasions when a few words will offer useful clues to the nature of the person or situation that you find yourself faced with. Those who give Tarot or spiritual readings might find this kind of quick reference data a useful aid to their readings as it can help them to understand their clients or the people in their lives.

For this chapter, you need to use the date of birth to find your Life Number. You can reduce this to two digits, as long as the numbers fall between 1 and 21, which is the range of Life Numbers our system of numerology covers. If the number adds up to more than 21, you will have to reduce it. Here is an example of how to find a Life Number if the total is less than 21:

Date of birth: January 2, 1970
Addition: $1 + 2 + 1 + 9 + 7 + 0 = 20$
Number 20 comes between 1 and 21, so it is within the range.

And here is one that initially adds up to more than 21:
Date of birth: May 2, 1982
Addition: $5 + 2 + 1 + 9 + 8 + 2 = 27$
Number 27 is outside the range, so we reduce it by adding the 2 and the 7 to make 9.

Here are the chief characteristics of each of the Life Numbers:

1	2
• A purposeful leader • Creative if there is sufficient opportunity • Likes to exercise authority	• Well-balanced and cheerful • Sensitive to the needs of others • Interested in partnerships, teamwork, and politics

3	4
• Versatile, adaptable, and easily bored by routine • Needs freedom to travel and explore • Intuition and common sense lead to success	• Hardworking, sensible, logical, and methodical • Can be materialistic and fussy • Either very traditional or a real reformer

5	6
• Lively, creative, and artistic • An excellent communicator who may teach or write • Loves travel, but balances this with home and family life	• Harmony in the home and among friends is vital • A hard worker who sacrifices himself for others • Can succeed in entertainment, writing, the arts, or the health industry

7	8
• Spiritual, sensitive, and intuitive • Into alternative therapies, psychism, and mysticism • Caring, but also attracted to film, poetry, art, and story-writing	• Ambitious, self-sufficient, and persistent • A powerful leader or tycoon • Interested in justice and honesty

9	10
• Creative, spiritual, compassionate • Interested in the theater and the arts • Can be religious, possibly too much so	• Self-motivated • Not easily influenced by others • The head of a family and king of his or her realm at work

11	12
• A determined personality who can get things done • High principles, but selfishness may spoil good intentions • Able to take risks successfully, as long as he or she is not too self-indulgent	• Emotional, prone to sacrifice • Associated with the unseen and secrecy • An uneducated person

13

- Linked to positive power when used wisely
- A reliable worker
- A home-loving person

14

- Someone who likes challenge and movement
- A rich person
- A reckless person

15

- A powerful person who may be into magic
- A lucky person
- A fondness for drama and upheaval

16

- This person finds it hard to keep to a steady course
- A passionate, volatile person
- This person may be an explorer, inventor, or just impulsive and rash

17

- A spiritual number connected with intuition
- Sometimes called the number of immortality
- The subject can overcome difficulties

18

- The person is fond of his or her home and family
- The individual can overcome difficulties
- The individual can balance material and spiritual matters

19

- Success, good humor, and happiness
- The person can be lucky and famous
- This person loves children

20

- Fate and karma rule here
- This subject is never boring or dull
- Good at making plans work

21

- Denotes power, success, and achievement
- Success and karmic benefits
- Persistent and successful

❋ ❋ ❋

9

THE BIRTH DAY NUMBER

This concept of the Birth Day Number is popular in Europe, but it isn't well known in the UK or the USA. It seems to work fairly well, though, so let's take a look at it. The idea is that the day of the month on which you were born exerts a modifying effect on your character. A couple of interesting side issues are that certain crystals are said to link with various Day Numbers, while particular fruits, vegetables, spices, and herbs are also linked with them, as you will see later in this chapter, but you must use common sense and take care with anything that you eat or drink, as it may not suit you.

Day Number 1

Born on the 1st, 10th, 19th, or 28th of the month

You like to be active and your mind is always busy. You may be a writer, journalist, or traveler. You are honest and active, happy and friendly. You grow and develop over time, which leads you to discard some old friends and make new ones as you go through life.

Day Number 2

Born on the 2nd, 11th, 20th, or 29th of the month

You are happier in a partnership or with others than on your own, but you do have an inner life, as you can be dreamy and artistic. You make a good friend and love to help others. You are restless and changeable, so you love to travel and explore new worlds.

Day Number 3

Born on the 3rd, 12th, 21st, or 30th of the month

You will be successful in your job or profession because you work hard and get things done, and you have leadership qualities. You have excellent judgment and can inspire others to succeed. You fight for justice for others. Being sociable, you have good friends who are there when you need them. On the whole, your life will be fulfilling and successful.

Day Number 4

Born on the 4th, 13th, 22nd, or 31st of the month

You are a rebel who seeks to change the world for the better. You are an original thinker and a person who likes to be different. However, you have a measure of wisdom and are therefore are not destructive for the sake of it.

Day Number 5

Born on the 5th, 14th, or 23rd of the month

This number makes you restless and unable to sit still for long, so you may be into sports or a job that gives you a lot of variety and change. Being youthful yourself, you get along well with children, so you are surprisingly good at family life. You may be keen on religion or places that are associated with religion.

Day Number 6

Born on the 6th, 15th, or 24th of the month

You are artistic, musical, and creative and you are deeply into these things. You have a sunny disposition, and love to love and to make others happy. Your hatred of raised voices and discord makes it hard for you to stand up for yourself at times.

Day Number 7

Born on the 7th, 16th, or 25th of the month

You are intelligent and somewhat psychic, but may be somewhat peculiar at times, to the point where others struggle to understand you. You love to travel and experience interesting people and places, and you may suddenly take off on a trip and then turn up again unexpectedly. You can put up with a lot and can sacrifice a good deal if it feels right for you to do so.

Day Number 8

Born on the 8th, 17th, or 26th of the month

Inwardly loving and caring and an inspiration to others, you have a kind heart that isn't immediately obvious on the outside, so you seem tougher than you are. You are ambitious and hardworking and can achieve a great deal, but you tend to overdo things and wear yourself out. You don't take risks as a rule, because you prefer to carefully consider everything before acting.

Day Number 9

Born on the 9th, 18th, or 27th of the month

You have a high opinion of yourself and will fight anyone who seeks to oppose you or demean you in any way, but you also stand up for those you love and will go to great lengths to make sure they are all right. You have leadership qualities. You are a reliable worker and family member, but you are also idealistic, so you may choose to work for the benefit of humanity or the future of the planet.

Day Number Crystals

Here is a list of the crystals that vibrate with your Day Number. There are many for each of you to choose from.

Day Number	Gems, Crystals, and Stones
1	moonstone, emerald, ruby, jasper
2	pearl, diamond, blue lace agate, clear quartz
3	amethyst, topaz, sodalite, tanzanite
4	tiger's eye, coral, pearl, obsidian
5	diamond, emerald, sapphire, citrine
6	turquoise, rose quartz, malachite, carnelian
7	lapis lazuli, topaz, moonstone, aventurine
8	sapphire, black pearl, amethyst, malachite
9	ruby, hematite, pearl, shungite

Fruit, Vegetables, Herbs, and Spices

Some people like to link numbers to dietary matters, in the same way that astrology links specific foods to certain signs of the zodiac. This can show how certain foods upset people who belong to particular signs, and a good example is spicy food, which can upset Cancerian or Scorpio people because they are prone to indigestion.

Please use common sense with things that you eat and drink, and avoid items that you dislike or to which you are allergic or intolerant. In short, the ideas listed below are only rather ancient suggestions that you might find interesting.

Day Number	Eat These	Avoid These
1	Citrus, apples, raisins, barley, cinnamon, ginger, chamomile, nutmeg, cloves, spinach, and honey.	Avoid fried foods and those containing lots of oil and fat. *never.*
2	Water. Watery plants, such as melon, cucumber, and lemons. Green vegetables, asparagus, prunes, apples, strawberries, and turnips.	Avoid chilies, too much spice, as in some curries, hot Mexican food, and Tabasco.
3	Cherries, parsnips, sage, parsley, mint, celery, beetroot, rhubarb, nutmeg, saffron, olives, nuts, and wheat.	Avoid getting overwrought or overstretched nerves, and do not work excessively.
4	Coconut, lima beans, small lettuces, spinach, bananas, and lentils. Also potatoes and root vegetables.	Avoid spicy or highly seasoned foods. You respond well to hypnotherapy.
5	Carrots, nuts, parsnips, cloves, peas, parsley, oats, thyme, caraway seeds, apricots, and string or runner beans.	You need to get enough rest and sleep.
6	Beans of all kinds. Most fruits, especially soft ones. Salads, nuts, dates, and green vegetables.	Avoid fattening foods, processed foods, and a rich diet.
7	Water and fruit juice, along with cabbage, lettuce, cucumber, celery, watercress, onions, endive, oats, honey, prunes, pineapples, and dates.	Learn to speak to trusted friends rather than bottling up your feelings too much.
8	Spinach, angelica, carrots, celery, marshmallow, turnips, figs, Cape gooseberries, seeds, and dates.	Eat poultry, fish, and vegetarian meals a couple of days a week rather than too much red meat.
9	Garlic, salads, onions, rhubarb, leeks, apricots, apples, mustard, and relish.	Keep alcohol to a minimum, and avoid rich and fatty foods.

❋ ❋ ❋

PART III
FORECASTING BY NUMEROLOGY

10
PERSONAL YEAR FORTUNES

You can use numerology to work out what is going to happen to the world in general during a particular year, but you can also find the number that rules your own personal year. It is a good idea to look back over past years and see what a particular number meant for you last time round, but it is never quite the same from one cycle of time to the next. We only use the numbers from 1 to 9 for predictive numerology, so the cycle runs for nine years.

One problem with this system is that there are differing opinions as to when a particular year should start. Some numerologists say it starts on January 1, others say it starts from your birthday. There are numerologists who insist that the New Year for numerology should start in September, but I have to admit that I have no idea why this is. For my part, I prefer to keep things simple and start the year on January 1, but the events might not kick in at the start of the year for those of you who were born later in the year. The most sensible method for working out when the new number starts to kick in is this:

1. If you were born during January, February, March, or April, take the number from the start of the year.

2. If you were born during May, June, July, or August, take the number from the start of the year, but also refer back to the previous year's number for the first four months of the year as it could still be exerting an influence.

3. If you were born in September, October, November, or December, take the number from the start of the year, but also refer back to the previous year's number for the first eight months of the year as it could still be exerting an influence.

To discover your fortune for a particular year, add the day and month of your birth to the year you wish to look at. Ignore the year numbers for your own year of birth, because you will use only the day and month. And remember, only the numbers from 1 to 9 are used for forecasting.

For example, let's say someone was born on May 6 and wants to look at the situation in 2022.

Calculation: $5 + 6 + 2 + 0 + 2 + 2 = 17$

Reduction: $1 + 7 = 8$

So 2022 will be a number 8 year for that person. Let's look at what the different Year Numbers mean.

A Number 1 Year

Astrological influence: The Sun, Leo
Key ideas: Fresh start, taking charge, making
    decisions, doing it your way

This is the start of a new phase that will determine
the pattern of events for the next nine years, so you
may now wish to take a new direction and even find
a new way of life. This is a time of new beginnings,
but it may take a while before the things you want start to fall into place,
especially if you were born during the second half of the year.

You will need to do things yourself now and to make decisions on your own,
either for yourself or on behalf of others, which may make you feel somewhat
lonely. You will need to put yourself first and also listen to your inner voice
rather than the opinions of others while making important decisions, because
your intuition will be spot on.

New people will come into your life, but old faces and old problems might
try to creep back in, and people from your past might try to control you. None
of this will work, though, as you need to move on and to have better people
around you from now on. You need to stand on your own two feet and have
faith in yourself and in the things that are important to you.

A Number 2 Year

Astrological influence: The New Moon,
    Cancer
Key ideas: Partners, love relationships,
    cooperation but also deception

This is the number of joint ventures,
relationships with others, and doing
things as a couple or as part of a business partnership, but these events will take
longer to come into being for those born in the second half of the year.

You need to be on a similar wavelength to others and to fulfill their needs
as well as your own. You may need to help people reach an agreement in
business or personal matters, and you will have to be tactful and diplomatic.

You may have to act as an adjudicator, counselor, or even some kind of judge. Partnerships are the name of the game this year, so others will make the running, and you may have to wait for them to make major changes to their own lives before you can make moves in your turn. There may be problems connected to love affairs or other relationships, and you may have to compromise more than usual.

There may be dishonesty around you, or people who seek to use you for their own purposes. You will need to be vigilant and rely on your intuition, because if you feel that something is wrong, it probably is. If you feel that your lover is hiding something, it could well be the case.

One benefit of a number 2 year is that you will be more creative than before, and you will have ideas that are inspired and original. If you are in a working partnership with an honest and decent person, these ideas can lead to great success.

A Number 3 Year

Astrological influence: Mars, Aries, or Scorpio
Key ideas: Sports, getting out more, creative ventures, and travel

This year will make you restless, either because you will want to broaden your horizons or because you will take a job that involves moving around and meeting a lot of different people. You will enjoy this era of change and opportunity, but these events will take longer to come into being for those born in the second half of the year.

You will be drawn into social events and may have to cope with public speaking, giving presentations, or teaching others in some way. You will need to pay attention to your wardrobe, hair, and general appearance at this time, because you may even find yourself being photographed for the media. You need to appear confident, so ensure that you know your subject thoroughly when you talk to others and try to be on top of your job. You will have business opportunities, but you could also have a small win or an unexpected windfall. This is a time of karmic benefits and gains, as long as you make the effort and don't allow time to slip away with no effort being made.

The problem here is that you could become boastful, too full of yourself or prone to exaggerate. You may spend too much or waste money and resources when you should be saving for a rainy day. Home life will not be as happy and successful as your working life, so take time to listen to others and make sure they are happy too. With a bit of effort, this could be a very happy year for you, and there could even be new arrivals in the family at this time. Work projects and even building and renovating your home or improving your property would go well, despite a few irritating setbacks.

A Number 4 Year

Astrological influence: The Earth; on a
horoscope chart, this is opposite
the Sun

Key ideas: Putting in the work, sensible budgets,
working with the earth, and recycling

Clearing clutter and getting organized is the name of the game this year, so you need to throw stuff out and make space for the new. You need to ensure that whatever projects you take up now are on firm foundations and are set to last, but these events will take longer to come into being for those born in the second half of the year.

Number 4 often relates to property, premises, and land, so you could be on the move this year, or improving the property in which you live or work. While this is bound to cost money, you must ensure that you don't get carried away with your desire for such improvements, so proper budgeting will be important. You need to be honest and straightforward in business and in private life and to ensure that those you employ are also honest. Success is on the way, but remember to be charitable once in a while.

Your feelings will rise to the surface, so you might become angry or upset at times and, oddly enough, your sexual feelings could increase, with an improvement in your love life. If appropriate, you could decide to start a family now. Partly because of the changes in your home, premises, and family situation, you might wish to put your affairs in order this year. This is certainly a time to attend to practicalities.

A Number 5 Year

Astrological influence: Mercury, Gemini,
    or Virgo
Key ideas: Connecting with others, sexuality,
    communicating, change and new horizons

Getting in touch and socializing with others, and mastering methods of communication such as new technology, are what this year is about, but these events will take longer to come into being for those born in the second half of the year.

You may take up some form of education or training, for a job or a hobby, and you will learn and grow throughout this phase. You need to keep in touch with others, contacts will become important to you, and you could find yourself involved in social activities or sports or busy with neighborhood events. Change is happening and you need to give consideration to your future direction and to making the right kinds of decisions. If you are fed up with your job or dissatisfied with your situation in general, this is a good time to assess the situation and make necessary changes. There will be new opportunities and a chance to find answers to current problems, but with the hectic social scene and parties galore, you could become overtired at times. The downside is that you might drink too much or get involved in the all-too-common drug scene. Take care.

If you have been single for a while, especially if you have been without a romantic partner for a spell, your love life will become more active now. If sex has been off your agenda for some time, it will be back again in a big way. You will be the center of your circle of friends, and others will like and admire you. This may not be a time for committed relationships, but take care with casual ones, as becoming involved with too many people will leave you physically and spiritually drained. You could end up becoming overwrought by all this activity, so you must build in time to rest. You must look after your health this year.

Travel will be an important feature in your life this year. Since this probably applies more to local travel than to exploring distant countries, make sure you have a car that is in good condition and that you can get to your destination and back again safely. There will be times when you need to be able to go off at a moment's notice.

Change brings growth, but you need to focus on something useful, whether a job, a home renovation project, welcoming new members into your family, or even having a baby, because without something to concentrate on, you could drift along and miss the opportunities for learning the new things that this year brings. This is definitely not a year for boring routine, and you may feel irritated by people or situations that try to impose a routine on you.

You may feel resentful toward those who seek to hold you back or keep you down, and this may encourage you to break away from relationships that are no longer fulfilling or from people who try to keep you down.

A Number 6 Year

Astrological influence: Venus, Taurus, or Libra
Key ideas: Family life, love and emotion,
    beautification, and taking responsibility

This is a year in which family and domestic matters take precedence, but these events will take longer to come into being for those born in the second half of the year. Your personal relationship situation might change, maybe due to falling in love or perhaps falling out of love. Arrangements with relatives, friends, and even work colleagues could suddenly come to an end, or they could change their nature. You may fall out with some people but also find others who are nearer to your heart. Note that these events will take longer to come into being for those born in the second half of the year.

If you started a new relationship during the previous year, this might be the time in which it becomes really important, and you could decide to marry and make a home together. On the other hand, some of you will decide that the partnership that you have been in for several years is no longer tenable. All of this could lead to legal issues and possibly also a change of address. Try to be fair when involved in disputes at home or in the office and avoid escalating difficult situations. Young loved ones and the elderly can be very disturbed by bad atmospheres, so try to be considerate where they are concerned. You might find this somewhat difficult, but there is an element of "doing your duty" around you this year, so doing the right thing by others will be more important than fighting to prove that you are right. You might take the role of counselor or keeper of the peace this year, while you attempt to restore harmony.

This number has a connection with image and appearance, so if you have been so busy that you have let yourself go, this is the time to get yourself in shape and update your wardrobe and hairstyle. You may want to update the décor of your home or buy some new dishware for your meals. Despite the possibility of disputes and separations, you could also fall deeply in love this year, and that could prove to be great for you.

A Number 7 Year

Astrological influence: Neptune, Pisces, or
the Full Moon
Key ideas: Retreat, restoring health, and
looking back before moving forward

Note that the events outlined below will take longer to come into being for those born in the second half of the year.

If you are in the lucky position of being able to take time off work or ease back on a busy schedule, you should do so now. You may be somewhat fatigued, so you need time to relax, meditate, and look back on recent matters before moving forward once again. If you can take short breaks, get out into the countryside or by the sea. Try not to push yourself hard and listen to what your body is telling you. Leave goals, aspirations, and major tasks alone this year so that you don't wear yourself out. Do the jobs that need to be done, but don't take on any large enterprises at work or around the home this year, because you will struggle to cope with them.

You could take an interest in art, music, or crafts this year, and you would enjoy a course of study, as long as it doesn't put undue pressure on you. You may take up an interest in fashion, antiques, or anything that enhances your life right now. Spiritual matters could fascinate you, so you might look into dream interpretations, clairvoyance, hand reading, the Tarot, and of, course, numerology.

A Number 8 Year

Astrological influence: Saturn, Capricorn, or to
    some extent Aquarius

Key ideas: Business and moneymaking but also
    strength, sex, karma, and service to others

If you have led a good life thus far, you can
expect to be in for a measure of karmic reward,
because you will gain in prestige, respect,
financial benefit, and more, but the events
outlined below will take longer to come into
being for those born in the second half of the year. Your career could take
off, and people who are in positions of authority could help you. You may
receive recognition for your achievements or, at the very least, an increase in
salary. Unfortunately, karma can work both ways, so some of you could face
unemployment and financial hardship and loss. Either way, there will be an
emphasis on money and the need for financial stability.

Intense sexual relationships are possible now, but in some strange way,
this could lead to you taking on more responsibility than you had before. For
instance, you may start a family now, or get together with someone who already
has children, and find yourself having to make room for them in your life. A
relationship may be extremely successful and may bring you great happiness.
You won't find yourself at odds with your lover or with the family, so you may
find more help and support than you expect.

You will definitely have to find a *balance* between money and material
possessions, love and family life, responsibilities, spirituality, and your desire
for freedom if you are to make sense of your life at this time. Try not to push
others around if you want to get the best from them.

You will have to work hard and could find yourself under more pressure
than usual or taking on more work than usual. Some of this might come from
an improvement in your position at work or even starting a business of your
own, but there will definitely be more on your plate. Oddly enough, you might
receive some kind of inheritance this year.

A Number 9 Year

Astrological influence: Jupiter, Sagittarius, or to
some extent Pisces

Key ideas: Spirituality, goodness, charity, common
sense, and the end of a phase

This year brings a nine-year cycle to a close, but the events outlined below will take longer to come into being for those born in the second half of the year. The last nine years have brought you good experiences and bad ones, and you have learned to cope with both. It is possible that you've experienced a measure of hardship, loss, and heartache, but you may also have grown wiser and more capable as a result. You are now older, wiser, and more in tune with the spiritual side of life than you were at the start of the cycle.

At this time, you can expect changes, so old friends and loved ones may move away from your area or just move on in some way. You may change your own address, change jobs, or leave an unhappy relationship in order to find peace. Sometimes we have to let go of people, places, jobs, or things in order to make space in our lives for new things to come in, and that is what is happening to you now. So you can expect to make new friends and find yourself in new situations as the year goes on. The best bet is to be open to new experiences and to go with the flow rather than trying to hang on to those things that are slipping out of your grasp. If you find transformation difficult, this will be an emotionally trying time, and you may want to get away from others and give yourself time to think about your circumstances.

On a practical note, you should try to work with others and spend time with others rather than being on your own too much, and you could do well to take up some enterprise that is good for others or perhaps good for your local community in some way. The feeling of being part of a team will make you feel less alone, while also doing good things for others will help you feel good about yourself this year. Charitable deeds and being helpful and compassionate to others will bring much-needed karmic benefits your way now and in the future, and new friendships can start to blossom.

❋ ❋ ❋

11

PERSONAL MONTH FORTUNES

You can check out any month to see what it will bring, or you can look back on a particularly good month or spectacularly bad one to see what was going on at the time. In theory, you could check a particular week, but you would need to count through fifty weeks of the year to find it, and that would be quite a chore.

To discover your fortune for a particular month, add the number of your day of birth to the month and year that you want to look into. So, if someone, let's call her Angie, was born on the 7th of July, 1998, but wants to see what the month of April in the year 2022 will bring for her, she needs to add 7 (Angie's day of birth) to 4 (which stands for April) and to the year, which is 2022.

It works like this:

Total numbers: $7 + 4 + 2 + 0 + 2 + 2 = 17$

Reduction: $1 + 7 = 8$

So Angie will need to look up the number 8 to see what her chosen month will bring.

Now work out your own number and read the interpretation that follows for the month that interests you.

A Number 1 Month

Key ideas: Individuality, making decisions,
    fresh starts, taking the initiative

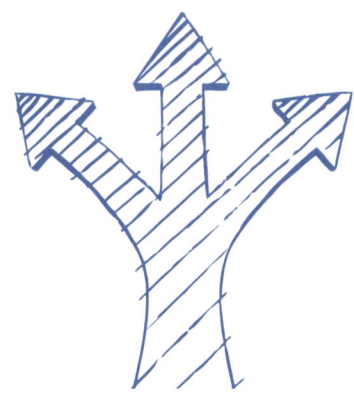

The number 1 not only rules the month in
question, but also signals the start of a new
phase, so it sets the scene for some months
to come.

Decisions and choices are in your hands
now, and while others might have something
to say about your choices, when it comes
down to it, the buck stops with you. You need to figure out what you are
going to do and what you want your life to look like in the future. You may
feel alone at the moment, but that is giving you time to go on an inward
journey and work out exactly what you want to happen next. Even if what
you want seems hard to get, if your intuition says it is right for you, have faith
because it will come about.

In addition to your own need for change, you may realize that fate is making
some of the running, and that you have to face up to some changes that are
happening of their own volition. This means you will need to cope with a
new way of life or make an adjustment to your current one. You may not get
everything off the ground just yet, but with the decisions in place, it is only a
matter of time before the changes come into effect.

Your job may change, and you may have to learn new techniques or cope
with technology that you are not trained for or not used to dealing with.
Your home life or family life may present you with new problems, and you
may have to find new ways of dealing with them. New people may come along
who can advise you or teach you new ways, but take care to only put your
trust into those who have your interests at heart. Those who turn out to be
good friends or colleagues now will stay in your life for some time to come.
However, self-reliance is the name of the game at this time, so you need to do
things yourself and do them in the way *you* think is best. You need to push
forward and be independent.

A Number 2 Month

Key ideas: Joint ventures, peace, harmony, and creativity

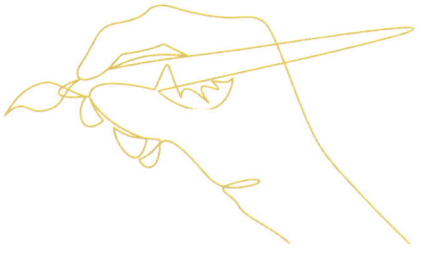

This number is about partnerships and relationships with others and the need to work in harmony with them. You may need to step back and focus on the needs of others rather than just your own needs, and you may even be asked to act as a counselor or an arbitrator for others. You may have to work as an agent of some kind, doing things on behalf of others.

The creative element of this number means that you could come up with some really inspired ideas, but this isn't the time to make major changes or even to make important decisions. You need to take a backseat to some extent and work out what is going on in the minds of others. Sit back for a while and allow things to happen around you. Romantic partnerships might go through a rough patch, possibly due to things that are outside your control. You may need to wait for hidden opportunities to emerge. If nothing else, tune in to your intuition and seek guidance from your heart.

If others seek to deceive you in either your personal or business life, you will soon know what the score is, and in time, you will be able to do something about it. Those who have hidden motives will soon show themselves, and then you can cut them out of your life or business affairs. Be scrupulously honest yourself, both to others and to yourself.

There is a good side to this number, though, which is that not everybody is out to deceive you, and there will be some who give you love, compassion, and hope for the future. Take some time out to relax, go for walks, do things you enjoy, and get some rest.

A Number 3 Month

Key ideas: Travel, liveliness, and creativity

Don't expect this month to be restful, because this is party time! You will be the host at a number of events and will shine even when the event is not one you are putting on yourself. You will have to buy yourself some new clothes and get your hair and body into shape for all this socializing so that you can "keep up with the Joneses." Being confident, or at least appearing to be so, will also help you to impress others. This could be an unusually lucky period with windfalls, lucky gambles, and business opportunities all around. Another happy possibility is of a new baby coming into the family soon. Just be careful not to overdo the bragging as it irritates other people.

Travel is strongly marked now, for either business or pleasure, or both. You may travel around your own country, or you may cross water in a search for new experiences and interesting places to visit. This should be educational and enjoyable. You will meet interesting people and be able to look at your own area and your own lifestyle from other people's perspectives.

You will have some original ideas that you can put into operation now, and your creativity will be on a high, but don't overdo things. Don't spend money recklessly or irritate others by being overly optimistic or boastful. The good life is all well and good, but if you eat and drink too much, you will gain unwanted weight. If you do nothing at all, but just trudge along without taking advantage of the social, travel, or business opportunities that present themselves now, you will miss out on what should be a very exciting time.

The only other downside is that you might neglect your loved ones due to being so busy enjoying yourself or wrapping yourself up in work.

A Number 4 Month

Key ideas: Practical matters, finance, legal matters, recycling, and sexual matters

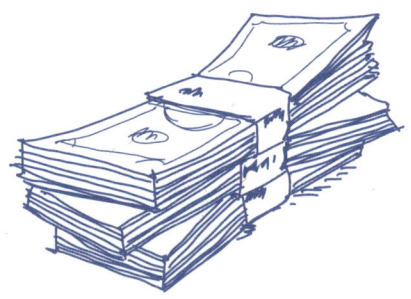

You need to look to your financial situation now and nip overspending in the bud before it gets out of hand. Indeed, this may be a somewhat lean month while you focus on getting your affairs in order. However, there is something that could run you into further expense, and that is the need to spend money on your home, not for purposes of beautification or décor but because it needs to be done, such as a repair. There may also be school fees or other family matters to pay for, so budgeting and cash flow are important now.

You will need to concentrate on your job but also to organize your workspace and clear clutter out of the way. The same goes for your home and garden as well, and if you can recycle or reuse things rather than throwing them out, it would be a very good idea to do this now. You will have an urge to spring clean or tidy up your life.

Your job or business should be successful for you now, but you must ensure that you are honest in all your dealings due to the fact that the number 4 relates to legal matters.

If you overdid things during the previous month, you may need to detox now, do some extra exercise, and pay attention to nutrition. You will become more interested in sex, and if you are in a happy relationship, this will make your partner happy too. You could even decide to start a family now.

The only real downside is that you might dig your heels in too much if any problems come up or take offense when none is meant.

A Number 5 Month

Key ideas: Local matters, connections, changes, communication, and unpredictability

Gaining experience and making contacts will be your most important activity now, and you will be very busy communicating with a number of people. You could become involved in something time-consuming in your local area—this may be due to your job or some kind of involvement in local matters or perhaps local politics. You will attend meetings, run errands, keep in contact by phone and email, make arrangements, and go to parties and social functions, so this will be a very busy time. Nothing will be normal this month, and you need to be ready for anything. This is the month in which some admirers suddenly discover you and you will be surrounded by them. You may travel more than usual now, so get your car serviced and check the tires.

Changes are in the air now, so you need to pay attention to your life and make sensible decisions. If you decide to change your job or your address, you can start to look around now, because you will soon find a better job or nicer place to live. If your relationship has stagnated, you might be able to enliven it, but it may strike you that the marriage or partnership is actually coming to an end. Change brings growth, but you need to aim for something and not just let life drift along without making an effort.

Try not to feel resentful toward those who seek to hold you back or keep you down, and try to relax your tense nervous system. Don't overdo alcohol or recreational drugs, as you need to keep your wits about you.

A Number 6 Month

Key ideas: Home, family, love, taking responsibility, and beauty

There will be more going on in your home this month, ranging from having work done on the place to people spending time in your home. You may have to cater for others and look after those who need help. You are the one who will take the responsibility for entertaining friends and relatives, caring for their needs, and giving the love they need.

The way your home, garden, and surroundings look will become important, and you may want to make improvements to them. You will also want to update your wardrobe and pay a visit to the hairdressers or buy new cosmetics or other personal care products.

If family members are at odds with each other, they may turn to you to settle their arguments. You are at pains to restore harmony to your loved ones and even to work colleagues. It is possible that legal disputes or legal matters will come to the fore now, and you will have to deal with those as well. Some of you will consider taking up counseling as a career at this point.

You might start a permanent relationship at this time and settle down with your lover in a home of your own. Alternatively, separations could occur and differences may become irreconcilable at home or in a business. If you split up now, it will be due to a powerful urge to achieve balance and harmony in your life. Justice will be important now, so try to be fair to all concerned. Do what is required at work and at home and don't make waves.

A Number 7 Month

Key ideas: Retreat and reflection, health
and healing

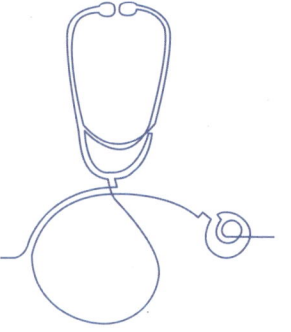

All work and no play makes Jack and Jill very tired, so this month you manage to get a bit of time to yourself to rest, retreat from life, and give some thought to where you are going in life. You may actually be ill at this time, and this is your body's way of taking you out of the rat race for a while. You will feel tired and you won't want to go to parties or entertain others. You need to be with close family and, better still, to spend time alone. If you can get out into the countryside or by the sea, this will help. If you can go horseback riding in a desert or look at wildlife in a local park, that will do, too. Do what you need to do and no more. Once you feel better, you might wish to take a class in an interesting subject, either to help your career or just for the pleasure of it.

Your senses are heightened, so you might take an interest in spiritual matters at this time. You may find yourself having interesting dreams or visions or simply "knowing" that something is true or going to happen. You may have spiritual visions or just take an interest in such things as astrology, numerology, and the Tarot. After the efforts that you have made in previous months and the effort you will make next month, this is a good time to concentrate on spiritual matters, religion, philosophy, and love.

A Number 8 Month

Key ideas: Work, power, responsibility, karma, achievement, and sexual matters

You will have opportunities for advancement in your job, and those who have specific knowledge or who are in positions of responsibility and authority will help and advise you. You will work hard now but you will reap the rewards for your efforts. It is even possible that you will learn of money that will come your way soon due to some legal matter or even as a legacy. Even if nothing this grand happens, there will be some extra money coming in.

The downside is that some of you will experience hardship at this time. The bills will mount up and you may not be able to pay them all off, so you need to work out a sensible budget for the future. Either way, there will be a definite need to focus on practicalities and financial matters. Much of this comes down to karma, because this is when you reap what you have sown.

Your love relationship should be very good indeed at this time, and even if you are both going through hard times, you will make sensible decisions and choices and work together to put things right. Number 8 has some connection to time and chronology, so you will both know that none of this can be sorted out overnight—long-term plans will be the order of the day.

Try not to become bad-tempered during this stage. Keep the peace and keep the faith in your personal, family, and love relationships. Don't try to push others around or punish them because you are worried or stressed. Do keep a balance between the material world and the spiritual world.

A Number 9 Month

Key ideas: End of a phase, change, wisdom, karma, friendship, and charity

In a small way the laws of karma rule this month, because if you have been working in harmony with karma and the universe, you will gain benefits now, but if not, you might experience one or two setbacks. Wisdom comes from an inner source but also from experience, and the things that have happened over the past nine months should have taught you some useful lessons.

In practical terms, this is the time to clear clutter, which could be a case of getting rid of things that jam up your home or workplace, but also the clutter of having the wrong people in your life. You may have to cut some people out of your life or stay out of the way of toxic relations. Opinions and points of view that don't work for you any more aren't worth having now. You might even start the process of looking for a better job, a better place to live, or a change in your personal relationships. You need to retreat from life and reflect on your situation, go on an inward journey, and give real consideration to your life.

Some people become overemotional during the number 9 times, or they refuse to listen or even try to understand what is going on. If you try to cling to those things that you can no longer have, you simply prolong the pain. Look to the future and set the past aside. You can't change what has already happened, but you could work toward a better future. Do some good for others, perhaps work for a cause for a while, and be compassionate and kind to every creature that you come across. Be charitable.

Friends, colleagues, and kindhearted relatives will help you to keep going during this troubling transitional time, so spend time with them now. Don't work alone—be with others and take advice from sensible people. If new friends come your way, embrace their friendship and enjoy it.

✳ ✳ ✳

12

A READING FOR ANY DAY OF THE YEAR

The following system will show you how to give yourself a reading for any day of any year.

The Life Path Number

You start by finding the Life Path Number, which is taken from your day of birth. For instance, if Sally was born on September 20, 1991, she needs to add these numbers together:

Total numbers: $9 + 2 + 0 + 1 + 9 + 9 + 1 = 31$
Reduction: $3 + 1 = 4$
Sally's Life Path Number is 4.

Finding the Day Number

Take any date you like in any month of any year that is past, present, or future, and repeat the process in exactly the same way as for the Life Path Number. For instance, let us look at June 16, 2023, and see what the Day Number will be for that date.

Total numbers: $6 + 1 + 6 + 2 + 0 + 2 + 3 = 20$
Reduction: $2 + 0 = 2$
The Day Number is 2.

Finding the Prediction Number

Now add your Life Path Number to the Day Number to find the Prediction Number for any day. For instance, if we add Sally's Life Path Number, which is 4, to the Day Number, which is 2, we get 6, which is the Prediction Number. So now let us look at all the Prediction Numbers to see what they mean.

Prediction Number 1

This number is the start of a cycle and a time
of beginnings, so if you need to deal with
something that is tricky, you will have the
brainpower, enterprise, and energy to do it.
It is a good time to make a start on anything,
or to sign agreements for future work. Talk
to others and listen to their advice and their
ideas, but filter everything you hear through
a layer of common sense. Do the same with
your own ideas just in case they are impractical.

Prediction Number 2

The number 2 is all about working in
harmony with others and also about
partnership and relationship matters, so this
is a good day to get together with others
and work out what needs to be done. If you
need advice, this is a good time to ask for it.
It isn't the time to start new things, but it

is a good time to continue working on current tasks and to get chores done.
Disagreements might arise, but try not to be overbearing or to allow others to
walk all over you in their turn. Don't keep going if you are tired—take a break
and rest when you can.

Prediction Number 3

You will be surrounded by people today,
and there will be meetings, discussions, and
teamwork. You will have some great ideas and
be able to solve problems quite easily. Do make
an effort to cooperate with others rather than
being obstinate or offensive. If others irritate

you, leave them alone and do some other job in some other place for a while. When you have finished work, this will be a good time for chatting over a drink with friends or even partying and having a good time. Some of you will take time out to shop for nice things for yourselves. Creative, musical, and artistic activities will go well.

Prediction Number 4

Practical jobs, chores, and household tasks need to be done today, but you will feel good once you have gotten them out of the way. You can work with others in a spirit of harmony and cooperation now, and this will apply just as much to doing things with family members as with work colleagues. Attend to details, but don't push others around while trying to get everything done quickly. Pay attention to lovers, friends, and colleagues if you want to maintain good relationships with them.

Prediction Number 5

If you have made specific plans for today, these could become disrupted because a changeable and unstable atmosphere is around you now. You may actually decide to do things in a different way now, which is probably a good thing. A phone call, email, or letter could surprise you and it could even take you out of the house or workplace on a kind of adventure. Everything is up in the air today and while it could be fun, it could also be a bit frustrating.

Prediction Number 6

You could take time out to shop for clothes and cosmetics or other products that make you look and feel better, while also taking a trip to the salon. Your mood is loving and romantic, so you might want to spend time with a lover, but if that isn't possible, you will listen to nice music, light scented candles, and do things that cheer you up. Naturally there are jobs that will need to be done, but they won't take up much of your time.

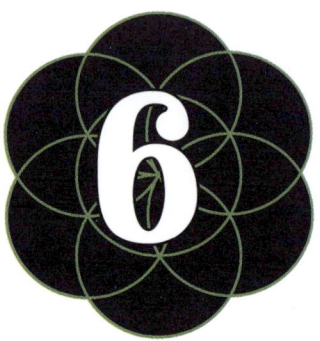

Prediction Number 7

Your love life and personal life will be on your mind today, and you may have to set other things aside while you pay attention to the needs of a loved one. This exciting day will be filled with love and, possibly in some circumstances, a meeting with a secret lover. Matters concerning love, passion, affairs of the heart, and relationships come to the fore now. Concentrate on your love relationships today

because something in your personal life needs attention. Oddly enough, there is also a need for you to contemplate your own life and your own choices and decisions to ensure they will bring positive results. Some of you will go on a spiritual journey while others will study something that interests you. There won't be much time for rest now, but try to put your feet up once in a while so that you don't get overtired.

Prediction Number 8

Tradition says that number 8 days are when people hear of deaths in their circle. However, most of these days are taken up with practical matters, and especially those relating to business and financial dealings. You may need to pay bills, sort out credit cards and bank balances, or work on a sensible budget. You are more likely to be on your own than with

others today, and you might want to focus on some problem in order to clear your mind. Consider the others around you, and whether there is some hidden agenda or hidden motive going on around you. People in positions of authority will be helpful now and business affairs will flourish, but you need to keep a clear head to avoid being used.

Prediction Number 9

Finish up any lingering projects or tasks, because a new phase will soon be on the way. You may want to check over things you have done and assess the quality of your work, but that is about all you can achieve now. Be honest in all your dealings with others, and avoid making major decisions right now.

13

HOURLY READINGS

You can check out a particular hour or perhaps prepare yourself for a particularly important event in your near future by looking into the numerical atmosphere that will prevail for you at that time.

This ancient system has far more to do with astrology than numerology, but it fits this book, so I include it here.

The table below shows every hour of the day in the left-hand column and the days of the week along the top. Track down and across to check which planet rules the particular hour of the day of the weekday that interests you, and then read information linked to the planet to see what the hour will bring.

Tip

❖◆◆❖❖❖◆◆❖

If you are in a country where British Summer Time or Daylight Saving is in effect during parts of the year, you need to jump back one hour during the summer months. You can find dates for BST and for Daylight Saving on the Internet.

The Hours (AM)

Hour	Sun	Mon	Tue
1	Sun	Moon	Mars
2	Venus	Saturn	Sun
3	Mercury	Jupiter	Venus
4	Moon	Mars	Mercury
5	Saturn	Sun	Moon
6	Jupiter	Venus	Saturn
7	Mars	Mercury	Jupiter
8	Sun	Moon	Mars
9	Venus	Saturn	Sun
10	Mercury	Jupiter	Venus
11	Moon	Mars	Mercury
12	Saturn	Sun	Moon

Wed	Thu	Fri	Sat
Mercury	Jupiter	Venus	Saturn
Moon	Mars	Mercury	Jupiter
Saturn	Sun	Moon	Mars
Jupiter	Venus	Saturn	Sun
Mars	Mercury	Jupiter	Venus
Sun	Moon	Mars	Mercury
Venus	Saturn	Sun	Moon
Mercury	Jupiter	Venus	Saturn
Moon	Mars	Mercury	Jupiter
Saturn	Sun	Moon	Mars
Jupiter	Venus	Saturn	Sun
Mars	Mercury	Jupiter	Venus

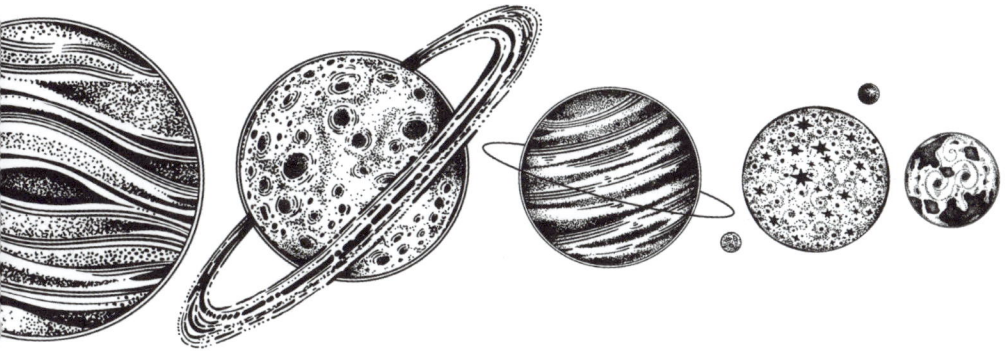

The Hours (PM)

Hour	Sun	Mon	Tue
13	Jupiter	Venus	Saturn
14	Mars	Mercury	Jupiter
15	Sun	Moon	Mars
16	Venus	Saturn	Sun
17	Mercury	Jupiter	Venus
18	Moon	Mars	Mercury
19	Saturn	Sun	Moon
20	Jupiter	Venus	Saturn
21	Mars	Mercury	Jupiter
22	Sun	Moon	Mars
23	Venus	Saturn	Sun
24	Mercury	Jupiter	Venus

Wed	Thu	Fri	Sat
Sun	Moon	Mars	Mercury
Venus	Saturn	Sun	Moon
Mercury	Jupiter	Venus	Saturn
Moon	Mars	Mercury	Jupiter
Saturn	Sun	Moon	Mars
Jupiter	Venus	Saturn	Sun
Mars	Mercury	Jupiter	Venus
Sun	Moon	Mars	Mercury
Venus	Saturn	Sun	Moon
Mercury	Jupiter	Venus	Saturn
Moon	Mars	Mercury	Jupiter
Saturn	Sun	Moon	Mars

Now that you have found the hour you are looking into and the planet that rules it, you can read the following to discover what it will mean for you.

A Sun Hour

Key ideas: A joyful and successful hour

Anything that you are considering setting out to do should have a great outcome if you make a start now, and any event that starts now should turn out to be a great success. If you are arranging a day or an evening in the company of someone you love, you will have a great time. This is a good hour in which to set off for a holiday or to treat yourself to something that you fancy. It is even a great time to make love, but alternatively, anything to do with children or young people will go well now. This is a great time to buy gold or jewelry for yourself or for a loved one, but it is also a good time to listen to music or do something creative.

A Moon Hour

Key ideas: Feelings are enhanced

Your emotions will be heightened, and you could be oversensitive at this time. You can't cope with people who annoy you, so avoid them for the time being. This will be emphasized if there happens to be a new or full moon today. This will be a good time for family matters, though, especially for cooking a nice meal and sharing it with people you love. Anything to do with property or premises will go well now, so make a start on do-it-yourself projects or household chores. If you can't even face this right now, go for a walk instead. Sometimes the moon acts as a trigger to events, so if you are waiting for something to happen, it should do so now. The influence of the moon could make you quite perceptive and even psychic for a while.

A Mars Hour

Key ideas: Activity and energy

Your energy levels will be high, so if you have something daunting to do, this is the time to get started on it. Anything that requires passion and commitment will go well, and that includes sporting or other competitive activities or time spent making love! On a less pleasant note, you could find yourself at the dentist or undergoing some kind of minor surgical procedure today, and all you can say to comfort yourself is that this is the best time for it. Take care not to lose your temper today or to start a fight for no good reason.

A Mercury Hour

Key ideas: Busy time, keeping in touch with others

Make phone calls, deal with correspondence, and sort out a number of tasks that have been piling up. You will contact friends, relatives, and neighbors now, and have some pleasant meetings with some of them. If you need help, these folks will gladly give it to you. You will be busy with the kind of day-to-day things that we all deal with from time to time, such as calling in a plumber, getting the car fixed, doing important paperwork, shopping for appliances or computers, or doing chores and running errands.

A Jupiter Hour

Key ideas: Travel, education, legal matters, spirituality,
and philosophy

You might book a trip or arrange to travel at this time, and this is especially applicable to long-distance trips that may be for business purposes. If you deal with foreigners or foreign goods in your work or business, this will be an important hour for you. You may decide to take up a course of study or to look into important matters at this time. If there is anything going on in your life that concerns insurance, legal matters, or important paperwork, this is the time to tackle it, and the same goes for getting up to speed with some new piece of software.

It is possible that you may go to a church service, perhaps for a wedding, confirmation, or funeral. You may spend a bit of time thinking about spiritual matters and even psychic ones. You may play spiritual music or classical music that moves you in a spiritual way.

In more practical terms, this hour could be a lucky one, so you might want to buy a lottery ticket or place a small bet. Business matters should go well, although there might be a step backward before you can move forward. As long as you are honest and fair, you should be able to reap karmic rewards at this time.

A Venus Hour

Key ideas: Love, affection, and beauty

Anything related to love and romance and even sex will go well now, so spend time with your partner and enjoy every minute of your time together. This is also a good time to indulge yourself by taking a long bath in scented water, warming aromatherapy essences in a diffuser, and sitting down with a good book or playing lovely music while taking a rest. If you are out and about, you might like to treat yourself to something nice to wear or to enhance your home décor, or even by buying some special food to share with your partner later in the day. Visiting art galleries; going to concerts or on a picnic or special date; or simply having a good time is a nice way to relax during a Venus hour.

In practical terms, this is a good time to set moneymaking ventures into motion or to set off on some business venture. If you are into farming and working the land or buying stock for a farm, this should all go well if started at this hour. The same goes for gardening, cooking, craft work and other gentle domestic activities. Venus is the goddess of love, so love and sex should be especially enjoyable now, especially if the relationship is open to scrutiny. This means a marriage-type relationship rather than something secret.

Oddly enough, there may be a reason for you to stand up for yourself, so if someone picks a fight with you, you will need to fight back hard—and win.

A Saturn Hour

Key ideas: Getting down to business and serious matters

This is a good time to deal with important people or tackle important topics, and father-figures could also be very helpful at this time, although you will be the one who makes contact with them. You will have to put a lot of effort into something for a while, but it will be worthwhile and may impress people who are important to you. This is a good time to start any difficult or long-term project or to make an effort to achieve one of your life goals. You may have to take an exam now or work toward something like the driver's license test, and you will be bogged down with finicky details or may have to concentrate on something that requires craftsmanship. Feeling overworked, overwhelmed, and overtired is par for the course now, but the results will be worth the effort.

You may have to pay a visit to a dentist or chiropractor, or you may have to pay some large bill, which means you won't have money to spare for fun activities until you have made up the shortfall. Limitations, heavy responsibilities, and difficult circumstances, and restriction may weigh you down right now, but there are always times like this and once the phase has passed, life will pick up again for you.

THE KARMIC
NUMBER

The Karmic Number shows where you can make improvements to your behavior in order to improve your karma and your soul's journey. If you know someone else's birth name and date of birth, you can spot their flaws and see how they might be going wrong.

To find your Karmic Number, take the Destiny Number from your whole name, as on your birth certificate, or, if this has never been used, use the name you were first called, then add this to your Life Path Number, which is made up from your date of birth.

Finding the Karmic Number

John Adam Smith was born on April 21, 1995, so we start by finding his Destiny Number.

The Alphabet Code

1	2	3	4	5	6	7	8	9
A	B	C	D	E	F	G	H	I
J	K	L	M	N	O	P	Q	R
S	T	U	V	W	X	Y	Z	R

J	1	A	1	S	1
O	6	D	4	M	4
H	8	A	1	I	9
N	5	M	4	T	2
				H	8

Total: 54
Reduction: 5 + 4 = 9
Therefore, John's Destiny Number is 9.

John's birthday: 4 + 2 + 1 + 1 + 9 + 9 + 5.
Total: 31
Reduction: 3 + 1 = 4
Therefore, John's Life Path Number is 4.

So now we add both numbers to find the Karmic Number: 9 + 4 = 13
Then we reduce: 1 + 3 = 4
Therefore, John's Karmic Number is 4.

Karmic Number 1

You can overcome a difficult start and make a success of yourself, even becoming fairly rich, but you must avoid being so materialistic that you forget the needs of others. Avoid bullying or controlling others if you want better karma.

Karmic Number 2

Others accuse you of being oversensitive or overemotional, but this is often because you are rarely in a position of independence or strength. Try not to trust others too much, and don't hand over your power to them or be influenced by their opinion of you. Don't try to earn karmic points by being good to others all the time. Forget karma—you have enough on your plate—so take time off, do things you enjoy, and try to relax.

Karmic Number 3

Avoid boasting and try to stay level-headed. Your energy, enthusiasm, and sales talents will make you successful, but your bad temper and habit of hurting others aren't appreciated and bullying never brings good karma. Try not to be impressed by those who have more money than you, and don't use others for financial purposes. If you want good karma, learn to be happy with your lot in life.

Karmic Number 4

Being stubborn and determined can be a good thing, but you shouldn't take it too far. Caution and unchanging ideas can be useful, but self-satisfaction leads to a fall. It is no bad thing to be a bit more flexible and to consider the needs of others. Being less proud of yourself and more inclined to help others brings better karma.

Karmic Number 5

You might be restless, easily bored, and uninterested in finishing what you start. You mean well and your heart is in the right place, but you may prefer to keep moving rather than put up with a mundane job or a restrictive family situation. You are not a bad person, but if there is a karmic lesson here, it is to finish what you start, be more reliable, and don't skip details.

Karmic Number 6

In many ways, you are doing everything that karma requires of you because you work hard, do a great deal for others, take on a lot of responsibility, and can always be relied on. However, fatigue and overwork can make you irritable and demeaning toward others. Try not to hurt others' feelings. One karmic benefit that you do have is the ability to make friends easily and to have good business relationships.

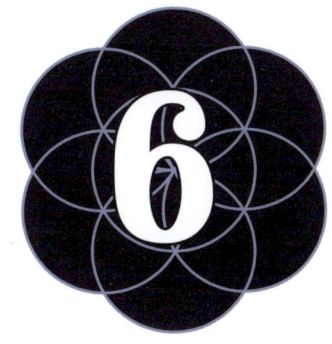

Karmic Number 7

You already know a good deal about karma and try to do the right thing, but you get tired and switch off from the daily drag of doing your duty. This habit of drifting and dreaming means you don't accomplish all that you can. If you want better karma, try not to neglect the needs of others or forget to pull your weight and don't fall into escapism.

Karmic Number 8

You take things too seriously. The world won't come to an end if things take a little time and if you stop to have some fun. You need to guard against becoming too materialistic, but you must take time to fire up the barbecue and enjoy holidays with loved ones. Try to calm down and not be too hard on yourself or others, and don't waste energy on focusing on the bad things people have done to you in the past.

Karmic Number 9

Let's face it, you are a bit of a loner and may be much happier to be among animals than people, but there are times when togetherness can be useful, especially in a work situation. You are good in emergencies and you keep a cool head in a crisis. Avoid creating upsets in the family, and act as a peacemaker if you can. If a friendship proves to be impossible, make new friends and move on.

✳ ✳ ✳

CONCLUSION

As you have now discovered, numerology is a really easy divination to work with, and you don't need to use all the different aspects of the subject in one sitting. For instance, you may be particularly interested in someone's outer nature but not concerned with their karma, or you may wish to explore someone's inner drives and motivations but not worry about their job prospects. There are so many potential sides to numerology that you will want to keep this book handy whenever you wish to look into a situation for your friends and loved ones or even better understand a person you dislike!

If a friend happens to be going through a particularly difficult time, it is worth looking at their monthly and annual forecasts to see when things will improve, because nothing stays the same forever—not even unhappiness. Or if you have an important meeting coming up, you can check out the day and the hour in advance to see how it's likely to go. However you use this book, I wish you the very best of luck.

ABOUT THE AUTHOR

When she was young, Sasha wanted to know what made people tick, so when she read a book with chapters on palmistry, astrology, numerology, and so forth, it started a lifelong interest which led to a career as an astrologer, palmist, and tarot reader. A request to write a stars column for a small magazine set her off as a writer, but it was a book that showed people how to read tarot cards that encouraged her to write her first book. Sasha's current tally is 136 books with sales of around 7 million copies and translations into 15 languages. She just completed the third novel in her much-loved Tudorland trilogy.

Sasha wrote the stars page for *Woman's Own* magazine for six years and for the *Sunday People Newspaper* for two years. She wrote a syndicated column for many local papers and she has written about 3,000 articles and columns for newspapers and magazines. She has broadcast on most UK radio stations, many overseas stations and also many TV shows, and had her own show on United Artists Television. She has given talks at hundreds of festivals in the UK and abroad. Sasha has served twice as President of the British Astrological and Psychic Society (BAPS), she is a former Chair of the Advisory Panel on Astrological Education (APAE), and she served on the Executive Council of the Writers' Guild of Great Britain.

Sasha is married to Jan Budkowski; they live in the west of England, and they have two children and four grandchildren.

IMAGE CREDITS

Illustrations by Terry Marks: pages 65, 66, 67, 68, 69, 70, 71, 72, 73, 74, 75, 76, 77, 130, 131, 132, 133

Geometric shapes © shooarts/Shutterstock: pages 20, 21, 22, 24, 25, 27, 28, 29, 31, 33, 34, 35, 38, 39, 40, 41, 44, 45, 46, 47, 50, 51, 52, 53, 56, 57, 58, 59, 60, 61, 82, 83, 84, 85, 120, 121, 122, 123, 136, 137, 138

All other interior illustrations: pages 7 © Everett Historical/Shutterstock; 9 © uladzimir zgurski/Shutterstock; 12 (numbers) © ileezhun/Shutterstock; 12 (crystal ball) © bioraven/Shutterstock; 13 © MoreVector/Shutterstock; 26 © Vecster/Shutterstock; 32 © GrAl/Shutterstock; 81 © magic pictures/Shutterstock; 91, 92, 93 © natrot/Shutterstock; 94 (bottom) © andrey oleynik/Shutterstock; 94 (top) © dariatroi/Shutterstock; 100 (bottom) © Jean Valjeann/Shutterstock; 100 (top) © Boo-Tique/Shutterstock; 101 © Great_Kit/Shutterstock; 102 © nikolae/Shutterstock; 103 © debay/Shutterstock; 104 © Andi Muhammad Hasbi H/Shutterstock; 105 © Leone_V/Shutterstock; 106 © Palsur/Shutterstock; 107 © kuroksta/Shutterstock; 109 © Alexandr III/Shutterstock; 110, 114 (top), 116 © dabradzei/Shutterstock; 111 © NikVektor/Shutterstock; 112 © ArtMari/Shutterstock; 113 © anon_tae/Shutterstock; 114 (bottom) © Nadya Dobrynina/Shutterstock; 115 © one line man/Shutterstock; 117 © Olga Kostina/Shutterstock; 125 © ArtColibris/Shutterstock; 126–7, 128, 129 © Svesla Tasla/Shutterstock

INDEX